Best Easy Bike Rides
Washington, DC

Help Us Keep This Guide Up to Date

Every effort has been made by the author and editors to make this guide as accurate and useful as possible. However, many things can change after a guide is published—trails are rerouted, regulations change, techniques evolve, facilities come under new management, etc.

We appreciate hearing from you concerning your experiences with this guide and how you feel it could be improved and kept up to date. While we may not be able to respond to all comments and suggestions, we'll take them to heart and we'll also make certain to share them with the author. Please send your comments and suggestions to the following address:

FalconGuides
Reader Response/Editorial Department
246 Goose Lane, Suite 200
Guilford, CT 06437

Thanks for your input, and happy cycling!

Best Easy Bike Rides Series

Best Easy Bike Rides
Washington, DC

Martín Fernández

FALCONGUIDES

GUILFORD, CONNECTICUT

FALCONGUIDES®

An imprint of The Rowman & Littlefield Publishing Group, Inc.
4501 Forbes Blvd., Ste. 200
Lanham, MD 20706
www.rowman.com
Falcon and FalconGuides are registered trademarks and Make Adventure Your Story is a trademark of The Rowman & Littlefield Publishing Group, Inc.

Distributed by NATIONAL BOOK NETWORK

Copyright © 2021 The Rowman & Littlefield Publishing Group

Maps by Melissa Baker

British Library Cataloguing in Publication Information available

Library of Congress Cataloging-in-Publication Data
Names: Fernandez, Martin, author.
Title: Best easy bike rides Washington, DC / Martín Fernández.
Description: Guilford, Connecticut : FalconGuides, [2021] | Series: Best easy bike rides series | "Distributed by NATIONAL BOOK NETWORK"—T.p. verso. | Summary: "Includes concise descriptions and detailed maps for twenty easy-to-follow rides in the Washington, DC, area"— Provided by publisher.
Identifiers: LCCN 2020052119 (print) | LCCN 2020052120 (ebook) | ISBN 9781493053919 (Paperback : acid-free paper) | ISBN 9781493053926 (ePub)
Subjects: LCSH: Cycling—Washington Metropolitan Area—Guidebooks. | Bicycle touring—Washington Metropolitan Area—Guidebooks. | Mountain biking—Washington Metropolitan Area—Guidebooks. | Washington Metropolitan Area—Guidebooks. | Washington (D.C.)—Description and travel. | Washington (D.C.)—Guidebooks.
Classification: LCC GV1045.5.W18 F48 2021 (print) | LCC GV1045.5.W18 (ebook) | DDC 917.5304—dc23
LC record available at https://lccn.loc.gov/2020052119
LC ebook record available at https://lccn.loc.gov/2020052120

♾️™ The paper used in this publication meets the minimum requirements of American National Standard for Information Sciences—Permanence of Paper for Printed Library Materials, ANSI/NISO Z39.48-1992.

For Pete.
You ARE loved.
#WSGFABR

Contents

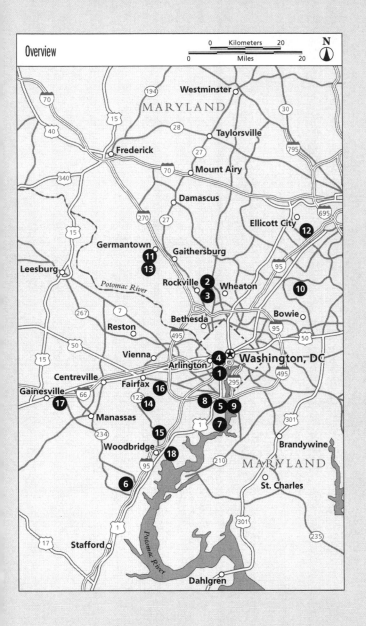

Honorable Mentions

Road and Pathway

Mountain Biking

Acknowledgments

It's hard to imagine putting together a guidebook like this without help. And that is precisely the case with this one. I couldn't have done it alone. This book would not have been possible without direct and indirect assistance from a multitude of individuals and organizations.

Every member of the Mid-Atlantic Off-Road Enthusiasts (MORE), especially the dedicated group of Trail Liaisons, who ensure we have quality and sustainable off-road destinations in the Washington, DC, metro area.

The Washington Area Bicycle Authority (WABA). Thanks to WABA, there are hundreds of miles of routes that can be enjoyed by everyone, and thanks to them, we have a voice that has helped turn Washington, DC, into a Cycling City in less than a decade.

Without the tireless efforts and encouragement from some individuals, this book would not have been possible either, and one rises above the rest, my loving wife, Courtney, without whom not a single word in this book would have been possible.

And to you, for picking this book up and setting out to discover the joys that can be found on two wheels, keep the rubber side down, and see you on the trail, or the road.

Introduction

Given the ever-present elements of expansion, one might think there are few recreational opportunities for the DC's residents and visitors. The city itself is home to one of the most famous stretches of parkland in the nation, the National Mall, where everyone may not only enjoy our nation's treasures but also take advantage of a variety of outdoor activities, including cycling.

Shortly after 1790, President Washington commissioned Pierre L'Enfant to design what would become the nation's capital. L'Enfant's plan consisted of a grid of streets traveling north to south and east to west that were intersected by wide, tree-lined, diagonal avenues. These avenues radiated out from what L'Enfant considered to be the most important structures in the new capital: the president's home and the seat of government—the Capitol.

Key to L'Enfant's design was a main avenue that would serve as a central axis for the capital. This backbone would be a wide-open space lined with trees where people would feel a sense of harmony with the natural environment. Today, that "Grand Avenue" has evolved to become an expanse of open space that welcomes all kinds of outdoor activities.

What L'Enfant did not envision was the evolution of DC's neighborhoods and suburbs. Long after he passed, the District of Columbia continued on a path of rapid growth. By the late 1960s, however, a series of racially provoked riots drove residents out of the city. That migration to the city's outskirts began a building boom that has yet to subside.

Today, DC is changing to reflect the interests of a new influx of residents. L'Enfant's avenues are seeing rapid urban revitalization. Streets that were deserted even just a few years ago are now filled with activity that is influencing a movement that has transformed Washington into a cycling city.

And DC's emerging suburbs are home to countless areas of open space where people can enjoy quality cycling adventures. Thanks in large part to the tireless efforts of cycling organizations such as the Mid-Atlantic Off-Road Enthusiasts and the Washington Area Bicycle Authority, the region has added an abundance of bike paths and trails, as well as designated bike lanes for both on- and off-road cycling, which have transformed the region into a true cycling destination.

How to Use This Book

The rides in this book were chosen by their best qualities to represent some of the best places for cycling in and around the Washington, DC, metropolitan region. I included downtown and suburban routes, open rides in the country, and a few traveling destinations farther from the city's center. All rides are within roughly an hour's drive of DC. Each route is introduced with the traditional guidebook fare of location, distance, highlights, GPS coordinates, and other vital information, followed by a narrative of the ride, including what to expect, local history, area bike shops and restaurants, and sidebars with bonus information. The following specs will help you choose which rides are best before heading out:

Start: Starting location of the ride

Distance: Miles from start to finish

Riding time: The time your bike is actually moving. Allow more time for rest or scenic stops, and of course for speed. Slower riders will naturally spend more time on the road than go-fast racers. Some riders stop for lunch, while others hammer start to finish, hardly coming up for air. Also bear in mind that severe weather, changes in trail conditions, or mechanical problems may prolong a ride.

Best bike: Best gear for the terrain—road, mountain, hybrid, or cyclo-cross bike

Terrain and surface type: A look at what to expect for ups and downs, and on what kind of surface (smooth road, bumpy road, dirt singletrack, etc.)

Highlights: Special features or qualities that make the ride worth doing (as if we needed an excuse!), such as cool things to see along the way, historical notes, and neighboring attractions

Hazards: Anything with the potential to disrupt your ride, like traffic, a huge pothole, a busy train crossing, or too many ice cream shops

Other considerations: Anything extra that is specific to the ride, like debris on the trail after a heavy rain

Maps: Available USGS maps from TopoView (https:// ngmdb.usgs.gov/topoview/viewer) are noted for each ride, along with any other worthy maps. (*Note:* The maps in this book are for general navigation only. Always be prepared with an updated map or accurate directions before heading out.)

Getting there: How to reach the trailhead from a major nearby location, including GPS coordinates for all trailheads

After the ride specs comes a few paragraphs of description that focuses on highlights you can expect to encounter along the ride. This is followed by the Miles and Directions, which is a detailed mile-by-mile, turn-by-turn description of the ride. This allows for efficient route planning, but your own variations (detours, rest stops, side trips) along with terrain, riding technique, and even tire pressure can affect odometer readings and skew the whole works, so consider the mileages listed as a solid, but not bulletproof, reference.

Remember, the real world is always in flux, and road conditions and trail routes might look completely different, or be gone altogether, in the time it took this book to make it into your hands. Mountain bike trails, especially, are in an almost constant state of rebuilding or rerouting or other modification. Always plan ahead and refer to detailed maps before hitting the road or trail.

Safety

Safety is paramount when practicing any outdoor activity, and cycling is no exception. While there are risks involved, it is important to recognize that it is almost entirely up to you to eliminate, or at least minimize, the chances of being involved in an accident. There is always the chance that someone else, no matter how in control or alert you are, may invade your space and cause a mishap, which is why you must always be vigilant, prepared, and aware of your surroundings.

The most important thing for you to do while out on the road or path is to be predictable and alert. If drivers can anticipate and have a good sense of what to expect from you, you will be safer. Making it a habit to obey the same laws drivers are subject to will help ensure your safety. Staying alert will also reduce your exposure to situations when the ineptitude and carelessness of others puts you on the receiving end of a foolish act.

It is not uncommon for an inattentive pedestrian hooked to a music player to harmlessly walk directly into your path and wreak havoc on your day. This also applies to you; if you love to listen to music when you ride, then listen at a volume that allows you to hear your surroundings.

In many cases, traffic-less situations, such as those you may encounter on the Mount Vernon Trail, will provide even bigger hurdles for you to overcome. The Mount Vernon Trail is notorious in this regard. On any given pleasant Sunday, you will encounter roadies on training rides alongside 5-year-olds on training wheels.

Off-road rides present a completely different set of challenges, yet the same commonsense rules apply. Mountain biking is only as "extreme" as you want it to be and, like on the road, you must also be vigilant and alert and able to hear what's happening around you. While on the trail, please make sure to observe the International Mountain Biking Association's "Rules of the Trail"; these can be found at www.imba .com/ride/imba-rules-of-the-trail.

Before setting out on any ride, on- or off-road, follow a set of simple guidelines: know your route, check your bike/equipment, check yourself, wear a helmet, and always let someone else know where you're going and for how long.

Ride Finder

Best Rides for Sightseeing

Best Rides for Water

Best Rides for Children

Best Rides for Wildlife

Best Rides for Singletrack

Map Legend

Transportation

═══⟨95⟩═══	Interstate/Divided Highway
═⟨50⟩═	US Highway
▬▬▬	Featured State, County, or Local Road
──⟨28⟩──	State Highway
───────	County/Local Road
▪▪▪▪▪▪▪▪	Featured Bike Route
▪▪▪▪▪▪▪▪	Bike Route
----------	Featured Trail/Dirt Road
----------	Trail/Dirt Road

Hydrology

⬭	Lake/Reservoir
～	River

Land Use

⬚	State or Local Park

Symbols

†	Cemetery
✛	Local Airport
⚓	Marina
✗	National Airport
🅿	Parking
🛆	Picnic Area
■	Point of Interest
🛉🏠	Ranger Station
🚻	Restrooms
○	Town
❶	Trailhead (Start)
🎓	University
❓	Visitor Center

1 The National Mall

This ride will take you by some of our nation's most iconic monuments and memorials. I highly recommend you do this ride during the early-morning hours, when crowds and the noise of autos en route to area offices are sparse.

Start: Intersection of Ohio Drive SW and West Basin Drive SE
Distance: 5.0-mile lollipop loop
Riding time: Highly dependent on your sightseeing
Best bike: Any bike
Terrain and surface type: Mostly flat, paved bike paths and the gravel paths of the National Mall
Highlights: Monuments and memorials along the National Mall
Hazards: Other users, Segways, and DC traffic
Other considerations: The National Mall can get pretty crowded on a beautiful spring/summer day. Bring a bike lock!
Maps: USGS Washington West and Alexandria, VA
Getting there: From the George Washington Memorial Parkway, take the Memorial Bridge to Ohio Drive to West Basin Drive. There is ample parking along both sides of Ohio Drive SW; bear in mind, however, that parking will be harder to come by the later in the day you arrive. GPS: N38 53.026' / W77 02.783'

The Ride

Washington's original architect, Pierre L'Enfant, envisioned a grand central avenue that would serve as a central axis and anchor all avenues in our nation's capital. In his plan, L'Enfant proposed several avenues that radiated from the capital's most important structures, among them the president's home and the Capitol building. His Grand Avenue would be a "place of general resort" and "public walks," a place that would represent the grandeur of the new nation and highlight the power of its people. L'Enfant's vision would never be fully implemented; however, his designs and ideas eventually took the form of the National Mall as we know it today.

When the cornerstone for the Washington Monument was laid in 1848, the area looked much different than it does today. The Washington Monument was erected on the waterfront at the confluence of the Potomac River and the Washington City Canal. In 1881, after the great flood of Washington, which inundated much of what is now the Mall, including the White House, the US House Committee on the District of Columbia appropriated $1 million to reclaim the Potomac. Silt was laboriously dredged from the river by the US Army Corps of Engineers, and then deposited west and south of the Washington Monument, creating nearly 700 additional acres of land.

In 1901, Senator James McMillan and the Senate Committee for the District of Columbia established the Senate Park Commission. The commission's primary mission was to restore L'Enfant's original vision for the Mall. The McMillan Plan was to nearly double in size L'Enfant's original plan, taking advantage of the "new land" that had been created by the Army Corps of Engineers. The new plan laid out the foundation of what the Mall would become today, America's front yard.

L'Enfant's plans roughly outlined a rectangular area that extended from the west steps of the Capitol to a portion of land extending west of the Washington Monument—not quite reaching the grounds of what is now the reflecting pool—which was then the waterfront. McMillan's twentieth-century plan extended that vision to include the White

House to the north, the Jefferson Memorial to the south, the Lincoln Memorial to the west, and the entire Capitol grounds to the east. McMillan's plan also took into account the surrounding areas, including parkways and other memorials and structures that would enhance the richness of the nation's capital and the Mall itself.

Miles and Directions

There are a myriad of bike paths, sidewalks, and bike lanes in the vicinity of the National Mall available for cycling. The proposed route below will take you past some of DC's most iconic monuments and memorials and can be easily altered. Please remember, in some cases, you will be riding near or entering portions of national memorials dedicated to the memory of our fallen veterans; for many they are considered sacred ground. Out of respect, please dismount and walk your bike if entering any of them.

0.0 Start from the intersection of Ohio Drive SW and West Basin Drive SE and head north east along West Basin Drive SW toward the Martin Luther King Memorial.

0.1–0.2 The Martin Luther King Memorial and FDR Memorials will be to your right.

0.3 Use caution when crossing Independence Avenue. Immediately after crossing, turn left onto the bike path.

0.5 Turn right along the bike path that parallels Daniel French Drive SW. The Korean War Veterans Memorial will be to your right.

0.6 Turn right on the bike path as you reach the Lincoln Memorial. From here, follow the path east as it parallels the reflecting pool to the World War II Memorial.

1.0 Reach the World War II Memorial. Circle right around it to cross 17 Street.

1.1 Use caution when crossing 17th street. Continue heading east toward the Washington Monument.

1.3 Turn slightly right to continue on the bike path as it circles the base of the Washington Monument to 15th Street.

1.5 Use caution when crossing 15th and 14th Streets. Continue east toward the Capitol along the gravel path.

1.8 The Smithsonian Castle will be on your right.

2.0 Use caution when crossing 7th Street.

2.4 Reach the end of the gravel path. 3rd Street and the Capitol lay ahead. Turn left on the gravel path and ride to the far end.

2.5 Turn left again to begin the return trip on the opposite side of the Mall.

3.4 Use caution when crossing 14th and 15th Streets.

3.5 Continue following the path to the right as it circles around the Washington Monument.

3.7 Make a slight right and continue west toward the World War II Memorial.

3.8 Use caution when crossing 17th Street. Continue following the path as it circles the World War II Memorial to the right.

3.9 Continue straight and ride parallel to the reflecting pool toward the Lincoln Memorial.

4.3 Turn left at the end of the reflecting pool.

4.4 Reach the opposite side of the reflecting pool. At this point the ride will backtrack along the same route to the starting point of the ride.

4.5 Turn left and follow the bike path that parallels Daniel French Drive SW.

4.6 Turn left and follow the path that parallels Independence Avenue.

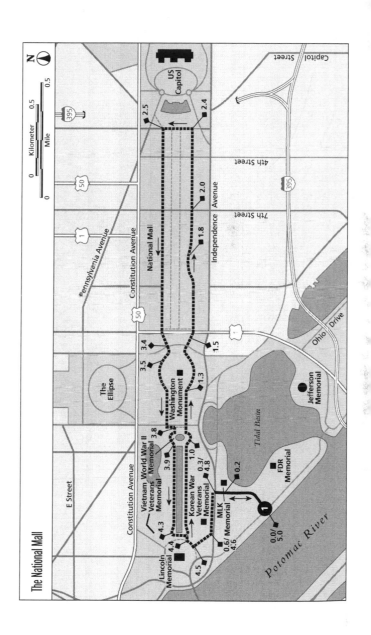

The National Mall

4.8 Turn right to cross Independence Avenue.

5.0 The ride is complete.

Ride Information

LOCAL EVENTS AND ATTRACTIONS
National Park Service: www.nps.gov/nama/planyourvisit/
events.htm

RESTAURANTS
There are often several food trucks along the National Mall,
but if you'd like to enjoy a nice lunch in a sit-down venue,
check out the **National Gallery of Art's Pavilion Cafe—
Sculpture Garden**, 7th Street and Constitution Avenue
NW, Washington, DC 20565; (202) 737-4215; www.nga
.gov/ginfo/cafes.shtm; or the **Museum of the American
Indian Mitsitam Native Foods Cafe**, 4th Street and Independence Avenue SW, Washington, DC 20560; (202) 633-
1000; www.nmai.si.edu/visit/washington/mitsitam-cafe.

2 Upper Rock Creek

This ride will explore the northernmost portions of the Rock Creek Trail to Lake Needwood and then return along the same route. This route can be easily shortened or extended by including more of the Rock Creek Trail to the south or combining it with the Matthew Henson Trail ride (#3).

Start: Winding Creek Park, Wheaton, MD

Distance: 10.6 miles out and back

Riding time: Up to 2 hours

Best bike: Road or hybrid bike

Terrain and surface type: Mostly flat, paved paths

Highlights: Lake Needwood, Go Ape Zipline & Treetop Adventures

Hazards: Use caution at all road crossings and stay alert for damage to pathways (potholes, washouts, big cracks).

Other considerations: The Rock Creek path can get crowded on summer weekends.

Maps: USGS Kensington, Montgomery Co., MD

Getting there: From the Capital Beltway (I-495) take exit 31A for Georgia Avenue North toward Silver Spring/Wheaton. After approximately 1.5 miles, turn left onto Veirs Mill Road and continue for 2.3 miles to Randolph Road. Turn left onto Randolph and then right onto Dewey Road. Winding Creek Park will be to your left as Dewey veers right and becomes Edgebrook Road. Park in front of the playground. GPS: N39 03.460' / W77 05.524'

The Ride

We'll head north along the banks of Rock Creek to Lake Needwood, a reservoir created to tame the mighty Rock Creek and provide flood control and protection for residents along the banks of the creek to the south. Lake Needwood also serves as a filter to ensure that water quality in Rock Creek is maintained by trapping sediment and storm runoff. Over the years that sediment has been dredged from the lake to ensure that water quality is maintained.

Strong rains over time forced the evacuation of nearby residents from the reservoir for fear that the earthen dam, which was built in 1965, would collapse and cause catastrophic floods downstream. The latest evacuation took place in the summer of 2006, when over 2,000 residents had to be evacuated for fear that the dam would give way. At that point the lake was more than 25 feet above its normal level. Fortunately for the residents downstream, the collapse didn't occur. Part of the reason that the lake reached such high levels was because it had not been dredged in nearly two decades.

When the lake was initially built, it was expected that dredging of its floor would take place every five years. Initially, park staff accomplished this task, but the practice was discontinued in 1990 as a result of constantly failing park equipment. For nearly twenty years the reservoir accumulated runoff sediment, and not until late 2010 did park officials plan for the dredging process to begin anew. The process to remove twenty years of accumulated sediment was finally completed in the winter of 2011, returning the lake, and the peace of mind of residents, to its original levels.

Miles and Directions

0.0 The ride starts from the Winding Creek Park parking area. Enter the trail between the playground and gazebo and ride toward the basketball courts. Head northwest on the Heron Trail, cross over the small bridge, and turn immediately right onto the clearly marked Rock Creek Trail.

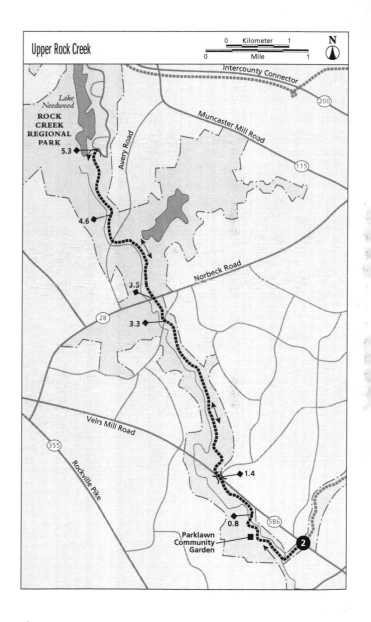

0   Kilometer   1

0   Mile   1

N

Intercounty Connector

200

Muncaster Mill Road

Lake
Needwood

ROCK
CREEK
REGIONAL
PARK

Avery Road

5.3

115

4.6

Norbeck Road

3.5

28

3.3

Velrs Mill Road

355

Rockville Pike

1.4

0.8

586

Parklawn
Community
Garden

2

0.8 Go over a small bridge and continue following the trail to the right. The trail will shortly cross the access road to the Parklawn Community Garden.

1.4 Go over the bridge that spans Veirs Mill Road.

3.3 Cross Baltimore Road.

3.5 Go under Norbeck Road and continue straight on the Rock Creek Trail.

4.6 Cross Southlawn Lane.

5.3 Reach Lake Needwood. Take some time to explore the area. You can continue to the left and ride the gravel path along the dam for some panoramic views of the lake. A right turn through the parking area will take you toward Beach Drive, restrooms, and the Lake Needwood snack bar (seasonal). You can also visit the Go Ape facilities for some fun among the treetops. This is also the turnaround point for this ride. Simply retrace your steps.

10.6 Arrive back at the starting point.

Ride Information

RESTAURANTS

Load up with some tasty pastries from **La Bohemia Bakery**, 5540 Wilkins Rd.; (240) 360-3697; www.labohemia bakery.com.

Overindulge after the ride with some Latin American favorites at **La Brasa**, 12401 Parklawn Dr.; (301) 468-8850; www.labrasarockville.com

RESTROOMS

Porta potties are available both at the starting point and at Lake Needwood. Go before you go . . .

3 The Matthew Henson Trail

This ride will explore the northernmost portions of the Matthew Henson Trail, a local neighborhood trail along the Turkey Branch, a tributary of Rock Creek, in Montgomery County, Maryland.

Start: Winding Creek Park, Wheaton, MD
Distance: Up to 7.0 miles out and back
Riding time: 1.5-2 hours
Best bike: Road or hybrid bike
Terrain and surface type: Mostly flat, paved path
Highlights: Neighborhood forests along the Turkey Branch, long boardwalks
Hazards: Use caution at all road crossings.
Other considerations: The Mathew Henson Trail can get crowded on summer weekends. Watch for errant riders, walkers, and other trail users. Boardwalks tend to be slippery when wet.
Maps: USGS Kensington, Montgomery Co., MD
Getting there: From the Capital Beltway (I-495) take exit 31A for Georgia Avenue North toward Silver Spring/Wheaton. After approximately 1.5 miles turn left onto Veirs Mill Road and continue for 2.3 miles to Randolph Road. Turn left onto Randolph and then right onto Dewey Road. Winding Creek Park will be to your left as Dewey veers right and becomes Edgebrook Road. Park in front of the playground. GPS: N39 03.460' / W77 05.524'

The Ride

The Matthew Henson Trail, named after the famous Maryland explorer who blazed a trail to the geographic North Pole in 1909, is a serene path along the Turkey Branch Stream in Montgomery County, Maryland. Our ride follows the trail eastward toward Layhill Road. Along the way we'll be riding on long boardwalk trail sections that hover above the forest ground. We will pass by tall oaks and a relatively new forest that was planted to replace trees lost during the trail's construction and subsequent opening in May 2009.

The trail runs along land that was originally slated to serve as a spur of the Washington Outer Beltway. In 1989, bowing to resident calls to preserve the corridor, 83 acres were designated as state park and another 117 as county park. Planning for the trail didn't start until shortly after 2000. Construction began nearly a decade later after public meetings and environmental studies were completed.

The trail's planning and construction survived strong opposition by residents and environmentalists in the area who feared that the trail would devastate parkland, threaten endangered species of plants, and bring all kinds of "unpleasant and criminal activities" to their backyards. Even the Sierra Club opposed its construction and at one point set up information booths during a parks and planning meeting in late 2001 that escalated to near violence. Thankfully, despite the opposition, the trail was completed in 2009, and the result is undeniable. The Matthew Henson Trail is a wonderful addition to the Rock Creek Stream Valley and the Turkey Branch. It offers a safe alternative for users and residents to link up with the Rock Creek Trail and a chance for local residents to enjoy the Matthew Henson Park, which until the trail's existence was underappreciated.

Proponents of the trail envision it extending well beyond its terminus in Silver Spring at Alderton Road to the south and connecting it with the Sligo Creek Trail.

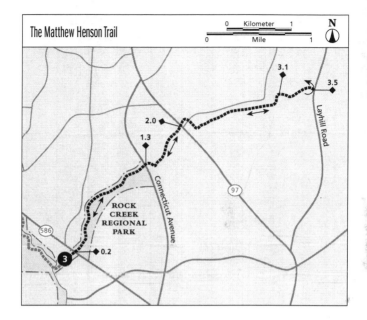

Miles and Directions

0.0 The ride starts from the Winding Creek Park parking area. Head east and away from the parking area toward Edgebrook Road; the first part of the trail will parallel Edgebrook until you reach Veirs Mill Road. The Matthew Henson Trail is clearly marked and easy to follow.

0.2 Use caution as you cross Veirs Mill Road. The trail picks up on the other side along Edgebrook Road.

1.3 Ride under Connecticut Avenue.

2.0 Use caution when crossing Georgia Avenue. Immediately upon crossing, turn right to head south on the sidewalk along Georgia Avenue. The trail will continue immediately to the left just past the bus stop.

3.1 Continue to the right to stay on the Matthew Henson Trail.

3.5	Reach Layhill Road. A parking area there makes for an alternate starting point for the ride. Turn around and backtrack to the starting point. (Option: The Matthew Henson Trail continues on the opposite side of Layhill Road for approximately 0.75 mile to Alderton Road, should you choose to extend your ride.)
7.0	Arrive back at the starting point.

Ride Information

RESTAURANTS

Load up with some tasty pastries from **La Bohemia Bakery**, 5540 Wilkins Rd.; (240) 360-3697; www.labohemia bakery.com.

Overindulge after the ride with some Latin American favorites at **La Brasa**, 12401 Parklawn Dr.; (301) 468-8850; www.labrasarockville.com.

RESTROOMS

Porta potties are available both at the starting point and at Lake Needwood. Go before you go . . .

4 **The Capital Crescent Trail**

This ride starts in a revitalized area of Georgetown, then travels along the Capital Crescent Trail to hip Bethesda, Maryland. You can turn around at any point and return to the starting point.

Start: 3255 K St. NW (corner of K Street and Cecil Place)
Distance: Up to 15.0 miles out and back
Riding time: 1-2 hours
Best bike: Road, hybrid, or mountain bike
Terrain and surface type: Paved paths
Highlights: The DC waterfront and downtown Bethesda
Hazards: Use caution at all road crossings.
Other considerations: The CCT can get crowded on summer weekends.
Maps: USGS Washington West, DC
Getting there: *From Maryland:* Take Wisconsin Avenue South toward DC until it ends on Water/K Street. Turn right onto Water Street and proceed one block to the intersection of Cecil Place. There is ample street parking along the waterfront and Water Street.
From northern Virginia: Take Route 66 east to exit 72 for Route 29 through Rosslyn/Key Bridge. Turn left onto Lynn Street and go over the Key Bridge into Washington, DC. Turn right onto M Street NW and then right onto Wisconsin Avenue. Turn right onto Water Street and proceed one block to the intersection of Cecil Place. As noted above, there is ample parking along the waterfront and Water Street.
GPS: N44 58.235' / W93 16.988'

The Ride

This ride will take you along a major portion of the Capital Crescent Trail (CCT). The right-of-way for where the trail stands has in fact existed for quite some time, and like many of the other trails in the region, it was part of a rail bed that served the Baltimore and Ohio (B&O) Railroad. Part of the trail parallels the Chesapeake and Ohio (C&O) Canal, but unlike that trail, this one has been paved and offers a smooth, uninterrupted ride from DC to downtown Bethesda, Maryland, and from there all the way to the border of downtown Silver Spring.

Plans for the trail didn't become a reality until 1986, shortly after the last run of a train on the B&O in 1985. During its heyday in the late 1880s, the B&O Railroad operated a modest cargo line that ferried building materials and coal between Chevy Chase and DC. At the time, B&O owners hoped to extend the line to Virginia via a new Potomac crossing west of the Chain Bridge to take advantage of economic opportunities to the south, but that never materialized. For most of its existence, the B&O terminated roughly in the area where our ride starts, but for a brief period of time the railroad was extended to fulfill an important role in the development of the city. In 1914 the line was extended beyond Rock Creek to the site of the Lincoln Memorial to ferry limestone and other materials necessary for its construction.

Beyond that, the line succumbed to the times, and over the years it became less and less necessary. Ultimately it faded away, making its last run in 1985 before giving way to cargo-ferrying trucks. The closing of the line prompted a group of individuals and groups to form the Coalition for the Capital Crescent Trail (www.cctrail.org). Its mission was "to convert the idle Georgetown Branch line into a high-quality, multiuse trail to be known as the Capital Crescent Trail." Other groups had their sights on the right-of-way as well, but ultimately, and after years of hard work, the National Park Service secured the right-of-way from Georgetown to the DC line, and Montgomery County purchased the right-of-way from there through Bethesda to Silver Spring.

Miles and Directions

0.0 The ride starts from 3255 K Street NW by the Georgetown waterfront. Head west on K Street until you reach the entrance of the Capital Crescent Trail.

0.4 Enter the Capital Crescent Trail and the Chesapeake and Ohio Canal National Historic Park. You'll basically stay on the CCT until you reach Bethesda. Look to your left and you'll see the remnants of the original aqueduct bridge that spanned the Potomac from Virginia to Georgetown. The aqueduct abutment is one of the only remaining signs of the bridge that preceded the now-famous Key Bridge.

2.5 Arrive at Fletcher's Cove. There is a snack bar to the left and restrooms to the right. Boat and bike rentals are available here.

4.0 Welcome to Montgomery County, Maryland.

4.2 Water, anyone? You'll find a water fountain along the side of the trail where you can fill up. There are a few others along the way should you need.

4.7 Turn right and then quickly left to grab the Little Falls Trail. You can continue straight here, but this section is a little more interesting and offers a nice view of the Little Falls Branch.

4.9 Veer left to continue on the Little Falls Trail.

5.3 Continue straight through this intersection; left will take you to the CCT. We're headed to Massachusetts Avenue.

5.6 Turn left onto the sidewalk along Massachusetts Avenue, and before reaching the tunnel, turn left and up to the CCT. Turn right onto the CCT to ride over Massachusetts Avenue.

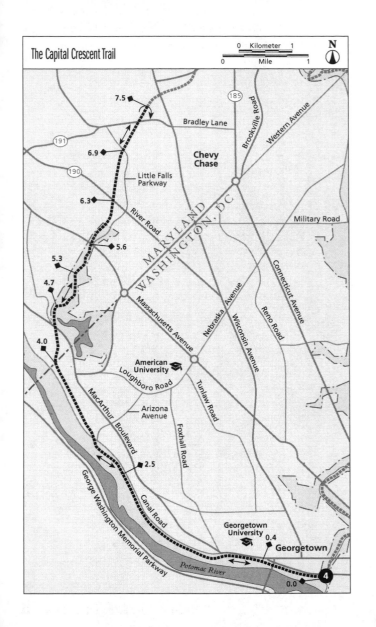

The Capital Crescent Trail

0 Kilometer 1
0 Mile 1

N

7.5

Bradley Lane

185

191

6.9

Chevy Chase

Brookville Road

Western Avenue

190

Little Falls Parkway

6.3

River Road

Military Road

5.6

MARYLAND

WASHINGTON, DC

5.3

4.7

Massachusetts Avenue

Nebraska Avenue

Wisconsin Avenue

Reno Road

Connecticut Avenue

4.0

American University

Loughboro Road

Tunlaw Road

Arizona Avenue

MacArthur Boulevard

Foxhall Road

2.5

Canal Road

George Washington Memorial Parkway

Georgetown University

0.4

Georgetown

Potomac River

0.0

4

6.3 Cross over River Road. The bridge was opened in 1996.

6.5 Use caution when crossing Dorset Avenue.

6.9 Use caution when crossing Little Falls Parkway.

7.3 Water, anyone?

7.5 Reach the Bethesda Avenue and Woodmont intersection. Turn around and backtrack. (*Option:* The trail continues on the opposite side adjacent to Bethesda Row Cinema. You can continue on the CCT to the Georgetown Branch Trail, but this portion of the CCT has been detoured to accommodate construction of the new light rail Purple Line.)

15.0 Arrive back at the starting point.

Ride Information

For info on events and other attractions, visit www.bethesda .org.

Taste of Bethesda, www.bethesda.org/bethesda/taste -bethesda

RESTAURANTS
Quick Pita, 1210 Potomac St. NW, Washington, DC 20007; (202) 338-7482

Mussel Bar, 7262 Woodmont Ave., Bethesda, MD 20814; (301) 215-7817; www.musselbar.com

RESTROOMS
There are no public restrooms directly on the trail. There are public restrooms convenient to the trail at Fletcher's Cove, near mile 2.5.

5 The Mount Vernon Trail

This ride allows you to explore portions of one of the region's most popular trails: the Mount Vernon Trail (MVT).

Start: Choose from one of the recommended starting points below.

Distance: Varies depending on starting point

Riding time: Varies depending on route chosen and starting point; as little as 0.5 hour and up to 3 hours

Best bike: Road or hybrid bike

Terrain and surface type: Mostly flat bike path

Highlights: Beautiful views of DC's monuments and the Potomac River. Option to visit Washington's home in Mount Vernon.

Hazards: Other users

Other considerations: The Mount Vernon Trail can get very crowded on summer weekends with riders of all ability levels.

Maps: USGS Washington West, Alexandria, and Mount Vernon

Getting there: Recommended starting points

1. Theodore Roosevelt Island (northernmost point of the trail) GPS: N38 53.785' / W77 04.019'

2. Belle Haven Marina (roughly midway along the MVT) GPS: N38 46.749' / W77 03.113'

3. Mount Vernon (southernmost point of the trail) GPS: N38 42.802' / W77 05.109'

4. Additional parking areas along the MVT are available along the George Washington Memorial Parkway.

The Ride

Built in 1973, the Mount Vernon Trail serves as one of several backbone trails for many bike rides in the Washington, DC, area. From its beginning at Roosevelt Island, you can connect with the Custis Trail or cross the Key Bridge and connect with the C&O Canal and Capital Crescent Trail—from which you can then connect with the Rock Creek Trail to travel into Maryland. As you travel south from Roosevelt Island, you can cross any of the main Potomac River bridges and access other routes around the city and into southern Maryland. If you turn west on the Four Mile Run (near Ronald Reagan National Airport), you can easily venture far into Loudoun County, Virginia, along the Washington and Old Dominion Trail (W&OD).

The route from Theodore Roosevelt Island to Washington's home in historic Mount Vernon is scenic, and no matter which way you travel it is serene—although the MVT can be crowded on a warm spring morning. Heading north from Washington's historic home in Mount Vernon can be equally satisfying. Riders can easily travel nearly 40 miles by heading south (or north) from either terminus and making a U-turn at the other end of the trail. But, if you are not willing, or able, to commit to such a long ride, you can easily park in one of many lots along the MVT and simply point your bike north or south to enjoy as long or short a ride as you desire.

Miles and Directions

I, like many, often pick a convenient spot along the MVT to start my ride. One of my favorites has always been Belle Haven Marina. It's at the midway point and has amenities that other parking spots don't, including a restroom, water fountains, and a great view across the river of Maryland, National Harbor, and the Wilson Bridge.

The marina, located just south of historic Alexandria, is owned by the National Park Service and offers, among other activities, boat rentals. From here you are minutes away from Old Town Alexandria, National Harbor, and Mount Vernon.

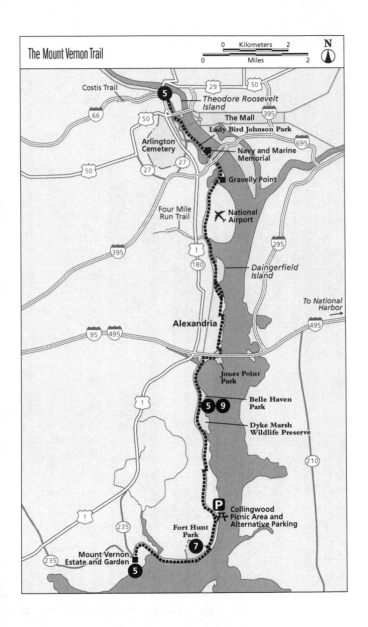

The Mount Vernon Trail

Costis Trail

Theodore Roosevelt Island

The Mall

Lady Bird Johnson Park

Arlington Cemetery

Navy and Marine Memorial

Gravelly Point

Four Mile Run Trail

National Airport

Daingerfield Island

Alexandria

To National Harbor

Jones Point Park

Belle Haven Park

Dyke Marsh Wildlife Preserve

Collingwood Picnic Area and Alternative Parking

Fort Hunt Park

Mount Vernon Estate and Garden

Once you park, head north or south on the MVT and then turn around at a point of your choosing.

Ride Information

LOCAL EVENTS AND ATTRACTIONS
Old Town Alexandria: www.visitalexandriava.com

Mount Vernon Trail: www.nps.gov/gwmp/mtvernontrail.htm

Historic Mount Vernon: www.mountvernon.org

BIKE SHOPS
Spokes Etc.: 1506 Belle View Blvd., Alexandria, VA 22307; (703) 765-8005; www.spokesetc.com

Big Wheel Bikes: 2 Prince St., Alexandria, VA 22314; (703) 739-2300; www.bigwheelbikes.com

RESTAURANTS
Lots to choose from if you head north toward Old Town Alexandria.

RESTROOMS
Restrooms are available in Belle Haven Marina at the starting point of the ride and along the Mount Vernon Trail at Riverside Park.

6 Prince William Forest Park

This ride will take you through a portion of Prince William Forest Park's scenic loop and give you the chance to experience unique views of one of the National Park Service's few remaining and best examples of a piedmont forest ecosystem.

Start: Parking area D
Distance: 6.2 miles out and back
Riding time: About 45 minutes
Best bike: Any bike
Terrain and surface type: Paved road, with one lane reserved for cycling and walking
Highlights: Prince William Forest Park represents the largest example of an eastern piedmont forest ecosystem in the National Park System.
Hazards: Occasional vehicles on the scenic ride
Other considerations: Take some time to walk some of the trails in the park and visit the visitor center. The park has several gravel roads and at least two trails accessible to bikes in case you want to add some "off-road" riding to your itinerary.
Maps: USGS Joplin and Quantico, VA

Park fees: National park per-vehicle fee (valid for 7 consecutive days) required. Additional information can be found at www.nps.gov/prwi/planyourvisit/fees.htm.
Getting there: The park is in northern Virginia, 32 miles south of Washington, DC, along I-95. From I-95 South take exit 150 west, VA 619 (Joplin Road), and follow the signs to the park entrance on the right. Proceed to the visitor center, where you'll find road and trail maps and additional information. Restrooms are available next to the visitor center, in the main Pine Grove Picnic Area, and in the Oak Ridge Campground. GPS: N38 34.730' / W77 21.893'

The Ride

The story of Prince William Forest Park goes beyond the first Scottish settlers who arrived on the shores of Quantico Creek in the late 1600s. A Doeg Indian community living along the banks of the creek predated the area's early settlers by thousands of years, but unfortunately dispersed after the arrival of Scottish settlers around 1690. A thriving tobacco industry flourished west of the then-navigable creek. The growth of this bountiful cash crop had an adverse effect on the creek, and by the late 1700s that growth caused the lands to erode and eventually fill the creek with silt, making it unnavigable.

The demise of tobacco farming saw the emergence of another harmful industry along the creek's banks. Gold and pyrite mines flourished in Independent Hill and Dumfries and became a significant source of pollution for the lands around the creek and the creek itself. Despite acidic water devoid of life, mine operations prospered and operated continuously until the 1920s, but falling prices and labor troubles forced their closures, thus ending a destructive chapter in the creek and area's history.

As the nation fought the ravages of the Great Depression, only a few small working farms remained in the area. As part of Franklin Delano Roosevelt's "New Deal," the Chopowamsic Recreation Demonstration Area (RDA) was created in 1933, and reforestation and reclamation of the "ravaged" lands around Quantico Creek were authorized. In an effort to reduce unemployment and teach job skills, the task of building what would later become Prince William Forest Park fell in the hands of the Civilian Conservation Corps (CCC). In 1936 the Chopowamsic RDA became a unit of the National Park Service, and by 1941 the CCC had built roads, bridges, dams, and five rustic camps for inner-city children.

Witnessing how the land has repaired itself from the ravages of tobacco farming and the destructive effects of mining is a wonderful experience. As you ride through the scenic loop, you can take an up-close look at the forest reclamation process in action. I urge you to not just bike this wildlife oasis but also hike some of the more than 35 miles of trails in the park. Along the way, in addition to the bountiful wildlife, you may even see hints of the early settlers who once lived here. Small family plots are scattered throughout the park and offer a glimpse at a not-so-distant past. Parking areas along the scenic drive make all these trails and features easily accessible.

Miles and Directions

The bike lane is a little over 3 miles in length and runs from parking area D to the entrance to the Oak Ridge Campground. In between there are two additional (alternate) parking areas, E and F. Our ride takes us from parking area D to the entrance of Oak Ridge Campground and back. If you are riding a mountain bike, you can easily augment this loop by incorporating any of the gravel roads, including Taylor Farm Road and/or Old Black Top Road, into the mix. Additional mileage can be obtained by heading into the Oak Ridge Campground or continuing along the scenic loop. Be aware, however, that continuing on the scenic loop will introduce several fast downhills and long, arduous climbs.

0.0 Start riding from parking area D along the designated cycling lane.

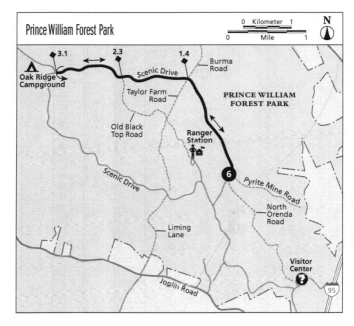

Prince William Forest Park

1.4 Taylor Farm Road is to the left, Burma Road to the right; continue following the designated bike lane.

2.3 Old Black Top Road is to the left; continue following the designated bike lane.

3.1 Make a U-turn and head back the way you came. (**Options:** You can turn right on Oak Ridge Road to head toward the Oak Ridge Campground area. This will add a couple of extra miles to your ride. Continuing straight along the scenic loop will extend your ride dramatically and introduce several fast downhills and long climbs. The scenic loop will circle back toward parking area D.)

6.2 Arrive back at the starting point.

Ride Information

Prince William Forest Park: www.nps.gov/prwi/index.htm

BIKE SHOPS

REI, 15200 Potomac Town Pl., Ste. 140, Woodbridge, VA 22191; (703) 583-1938; www.rei.com

Bull Run Bicycles, 10458 Dumfries Rd., City of Manassas, VA 20110; (703) 335-6131; www.bullrunbicycles.com

RESTAURANTS

Prince William Forest Park lies in close proximity to Stonebridge at Potomac Town Center, where you can find multiple restaurants and shops. Some of my favorites are **Brixx**, **BurgerFi**, **Potbelly Sandwich Shop**, and **Sushi Jin Next Door**.

7 Fort Hunt

Often overlooked by Mount Vernon Trail cyclists, Fort Hunt offers riders traveling along the Mount Vernon Trail an opportunity to add a little distance to their rides, or, as in this case, serves as a destination for an easy spin on a parcel full of historical significance.

Start: Parking area A
Distance: 1.3-mile loop with optional 0.7-mile loop
Riding time: About 45 minutes
Best bike: Road or hybrid bike
Terrain and surface type: Flat, paved park road; mostly one-way
Highlights: Old military batteries
Hazards: Minimal vehicle traffic, other users, hikers
Other considerations: Park can be crowded in the spring and summer months; pay special attention to traffic during those times.

Maps: USGS Mount Vernon Quadrangle, VA/MD
Getting there: From Old Town Alexandria drive south on Washington Street and continue onto the George Washington Memorial Parkway. Take the exit for Fort Hunt Park and follow signs into the park. If you are on the Mount Vernon Trail, turn onto Fort Hunt Road and follow signs into the park. GPS: N44 58.235' / W93 16.988'

The Ride

Fort Hunt, located near the shores of the Potomac River in Fairfax County, Virginia, has seen multiple transformations over its history. The park was originally part of George Washington's Mount Vernon estate and today is part of the National Park Service's George Washington Memorial Parkway corridor.

Beyond being part of our first president's estate, Fort Hunt became a significant military installation when it was acquired by the federal government in the early 1890s to provide a companion naval defense system to Maryland's Fort Washington, directly across the river. Both fortifications were erected where the river channel narrowed to help protect the nation's capital from incoming enemy vessels. Several concrete gun emplacements, still visible today, were built for that function and represent early uses of concrete for construction. These, however, quickly became obsolete, a testament to the rapid evolution and development of modern warfare. Sadly, these emplacements are closed to the public since they were lined with asbestos and pose a public health risk. You can, however, explore them from the outside.

The fort's military function ceased in the early 1930s during the peak of the Great Depression, when it was transformed into a Civilian Conservation Corps (CCC) camp. CCC crews from Fort Hunt would work on projects not only at the fort, but also in and around the Washington, DC, area. Among the projects carried out by Fort Hunt CCC crews were the excavation of a lake bed, a geographical feature still in place today, and various improvements to make Fort Hunt a recreational destination with a cover of woodland and occasional open fields.

Today, a loop road circles the park's central area, which includes multiple open playing fields and picnic areas. Our ride makes use of this lightly traveled road and the designated bike/walking lane, similar to the one along the scenic loop at Prince William Forest Park in Prince William County, Virginia (see Ride 6), available for riders of all skill levels.

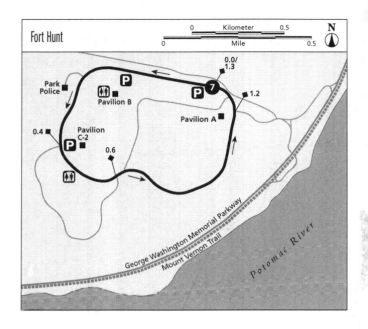

Miles and Directions

0.0 Turn left onto the Fort Hunt Park Loop. A short portion of the road will be two-way before it turns into one way. You will be traveling counterclockwise along the Fort Hunt Park Loop. The loop is continuous, with no turns.

0.4 Continue straight along the Fort Hunt Park Loop. (*Option:* A right turn here gives you access to a shorter loop in the park where no vehicle traffic is allowed.)

0.6 Continue straight along the Fort Hunt Park Loop. If you chose to venture onto the optional short loop, this is where you would come out.

1.2 Follow the road to the left past the stop sign, a right turn which would take you out of the park. Traffic is two-way beyond the stop sign.

1.3 Arrive back at parking area A.

Ride Information

LOCAL EVENTS AND ATTRACTIONS
Old Town Alexandria: www.visitalexandriava.com

Mount Vernon Park: www.nps.gov/gwmp/planyourvisit/forthunt.htm

Historic Mount Vernon: www.mountvernon.org

BIKE SHOPS
Spokes Etc., 1506 Belle View Blvd., Alexandria, VA 22307; (703) 765-8005; www.spokesetc.com

Big Wheel Bikes, 2 Prince St., Alexandria, VA 22314; (703) 739-2300; www.bigwheelbikes.com

RESTAURANTS
Lots to choose from if you head north toward Old Town Alexandria.

RESTROOMS
Restrooms are available in the park.

8 Holmes Run and Dora Kelley Park

This short ride will take you along Holmes Run, a stream in the Cameron Run watershed, and into a serene and secluded park in the middle of one of the region's most populated areas.

Start: Cameron Run Regional Park

Distance: 6.6 miles out and back

Riding time: 1–1.5 hours

Best bike: Road or hybrid bike

Terrain and surface type: Mostly flat, paved pathways

Highlights: The underpass at I-395, Dora Kelley Park, Cameron Run Regional Park

Hazards: Use caution at the Beauregard Street crossing. Do not attempt this ride during or after heavy rains; the underpass under I-395 floods.

Other considerations: The underpass under I-395 also serves as a water conduit and can be potentially dangerous after heavy rains.

Maps: USGS Alexandria and Annandale, VA

Getting there: From I-495, take exit 174 to the Eisenhower Connector. Follow the signs for Great Waves Waterpark. Park at the Cameron Run Regional Park parking area. GPS: N38 48.265' / W77 06.112'

The Ride

When I first moved to the area, back in the late 1970s, Alexandria seemed like such a faraway place. We lived in Montgomery County, Maryland, and only made the trek down the Beltway to Old Town a couple of times a year. Back then all I really knew of Alexandria was the historic portion of the city. It wasn't until I returned to the area in the early 1990s that I began to discover the rest of Alexandria, the third most densely populated city in the United States.

Back then we lived in an area that straddled Arlington and Alexandria called Arlandia. It was from there that I started to visit and discover the rest of the city. Our ride will take you alongside one of the city's rushing streams and into a secluded section of parkland.

The ride starts in one of the most popular parks in Alexandria, Cameron Run Regional Park, home of Great Waves Waterpark. Not long ago the area was nothing more than an unflattering industrial zone. Nothing much grew in the surroundings of the floodplain of Cameron Run and Holmes Run, and no one lived there. That all changed in the mid-1980s with the creation of Cook Lake, a small lake that serves as the backdrop for the park and where locals can go for some "urban" fishing. With the lake came new trees, homes, and eventually a new trail that runs along Holmes Run toward Baileys Crossroads in Arlington. Our ride will run along this trail, which is one of the most interesting in the region.

As you enter Holmes Run from Eisenhower Avenue, the landscape will turn somewhat surreal. Because of the surroundings, this section of Holmes Run has retained the industrial feel of its past. The landscape of nearby bridges and the large concrete tunnels that channel Holmes Run's water give it a postapocalyptic feel. That feeling continues as you reach I-395 and ride under the Van Dorn overpasses and then through the I-395 tunnel, one of the most interesting sections of trail in the region. As you exit the tunnel, the concrete surroundings give way to a tree-covered trail and a totally different feel. Last time I rode here, I came out of the tunnel and encountered a family of deer. It was like being transported to a different world. Holmes Run continues, eventually turning into the Dora Kelley Nature Park, a small stretch of land that is a gem in the area.

It's quite remarkable how a park like this shields you from the surrounding neighborhoods. The park would not have been possible if not for Mrs. Dora Kelley, a local Alexandria City resident who fought hard to maintain and preserve the woodlands near her home. Her dream became a reality in 1973 when the City of Alexandria acquired nearly 26 acres of land for the establishment of a nature park and wildlife sanctuary. The acquired land became part of a 50-acre parcel that now includes oak-hickory forests, a stream and flood-plain, a freshwater marsh, and a variety of native plants and wildlife not found anywhere else in the city. For her efforts the Alexandria City Council passed a resolution in 1976 to name the area after Mrs. Kelley, recognizing the outstanding contribution she made to preserve the character of the area.

Miles and Directions

0.0 Start at the Cameron Run Regional Park parking lot. We'll start measuring at the entrance to the lot in front of the park sign. Head west on the paved bike trail that runs parallel to Eisenhower Avenue.

0.2 Follow the trail to the right away from Eisenhower Avenue and alongside Holmes Run. Continue staying to the right at the next intersection.

0.7 Immediately before you reach the playground, make a left turn and then an immediate right to continue on the trail along Holmes Run.

0.9 Turn left to enter Holmes Run Park.

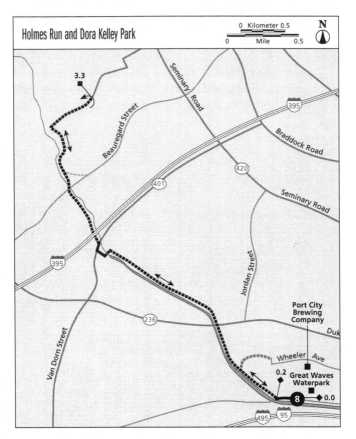

1.8 Turn left at this intersection to follow the scenic trail, not the urban trail. You'll go over Holmes Run and then turn right again. Note that after heavy rains this section of trail may be difficult to ride.

1.9 Go under Van Dorn Street and then through the tunnel that goes under I-395. Yell through the tunnel; I do.

2.4 Cross Beauregard Street and then hop on the sidewalk on the right on Morgan Street to pick up the trail that enters the

Dora Kelley Nature Park. This is a surprising little oasis amid the suburban sprawl.

2.5 Cross Holmes Run again and turn left to continue following the concrete-paved path.

2.8 Continue straight through this intersection.

2.9 Turn right onto Chambliss Street.

3.0 Continue straight onto the bike path.

3.3 Reach the perimeter of the Dora Kelley Nature Park. Turn around and backtrack.

6.6 Arrive back at the starting point.

Ride Information

LOCAL EVENTS AND ATTRACTIONS

Visit the Old Town Alexandria website for information and links about upcoming events at www.visitalexandriava.com. Two of my favorite Old Town Events are the annual **Saint Patrick's Day Celebration and Parade** and the September open-air **Arts Festival**.

RESTAURANTS

Port City Brewing Company, 3950 Wheeler Ave., Alexandria, VA 22304; (703) 797-2739; www.portcitybrewing.com

Sardi's Pollo a La Brasa, 1480 N. Beauregard St., Alexandria, VA 22311; (571) 444-7295; www.sardischicken.com

More to choose from if you head east to Old Town Alexandria.

⑨ The Wilson Bridge and National Harbor

This ride will take you over the Woodrow Wilson Bridge to one of Maryland's newest and most thriving attractions: National Harbor. Along the way we'll ride along both banks of the Potomac where the river begins its journey to the Chesapeake Bay.

Start: Belle Haven Marina
Distance: 7.4 miles out and back
Riding time: 1–2 hours, longer if you hang out at National Harbor
Best bike: Any bike
Terrain and surface type: Paved bike paths and a short section of road while you explore National Harbor
Highlights: Jones Point Park, the Woodrow Wilson Bridge, National Harbor, and *The Awakening* statue
Hazards: Other trail users and vehicle traffic in National Harbor
Other considerations: Bring a bike lock; you'll want to lock your bike and explore National Harbor on foot.
Maps: USGS Alexandria, VA
Getting there: *From Virginia:* Take the Capital Beltway (I-495) to exit

1, headed south on Richmond Highway (US 1). Once on US 1, stay in the right lane to take the exit for Fort Hunt Road. Follow Fort Hunt Road for 1.1 miles and turn left onto Belle View Boulevard. At the end of Belle View Boulevard, turn left onto the George Washington Parkway. Turn right into the Belle Haven Marina and then immediately left toward the parking areas.

From Maryland: Take the local lanes of the Capital Beltway (I-495) over the Woodrow Wilson Bridge and take the first exit toward Mount Vernon. Merge onto Church Street and then make an immediate right onto Washington Street. Cross the Washington Street Deck (bridge over I-495) and you'll be on the George Washington (GW) Parkway. Drive

1.25 miles and turn left into
Belle Haven Marina. Immediately
turn left again toward the parking

areas. GPS: N38 46.749' / W77
03.113'

The Ride

Just a little over a decade ago, this ride and its destination in
Prince George's County, Maryland, would have been impossible—largely in part because the old Wilson bridge and
subsequent replacement did not include a cycling path, but
also because the destination itself, National Harbor, didn't
exist. Both projects were in the making for several years. The
construction of the new Wilson Bridge was a necessity for
the region. Traffic along the old span linking Maryland and
Virginia over the Potomac River in the vicinity of Old Town
Alexandria often slowed down to a painful crawl, and it was a
source of constant frustration for area residents and an ever-
increasing number of commuters. In addition, the nearly
forty-year-old span was in disrepair, and because of the added
traffic using its spans, it was considered a safety hazard.

The bridge, which was originally built between 1958 and
1961 at a cost of nearly $15 million, wasn't supposed to carry
the traffic it ultimately did over the years. Its original main
function was to connect the communities of Alexandria,
Virginia, and Oxon Hill, Maryland, but with the completion
of the Capital Beltway and the exponential growth of the
region, the bridge was quickly outgrown.

Construction on the new bridge was initiated in early
2000 and included various stages, the first of which was
dredging the Potomac to make room for a channel to build
the first, southbound six-lane span. The plan called for this
effort to be completed first so that traffic from the existing
bridge could be diverted to the new span. The first of the

twin spans was open to traffic in 2006 and the second in 2008, culminating nearly a decade of construction. Sadly, no bike path was included. It wasn't until June 2009 that cyclists were able to cross the 1.1-mile span, but still, there was no destination other than just the other side.

The culmination of the bridge project coincided and spurred the creation of a new resort-like waterfront project in an undeveloped tract of prime real estate along the Potomac River and within view of Alexandria and the new bridge. The development was anchored by a hotel and convention center and ultimately the MGM National Harbor. Today, National Harbor is a thriving commercial and entertainment center with a multitude of attractions for visitors of all ages.

Miles and Directions

0.0 Start on the Mount Vernon Trail in the Belle Haven Marina in front of the restrooms and the Jones Point Historic Marker. Head north on the Mount Vernon Trail.

1.0 Cross the street and continue over the Washington Street Deck. Do not turn right at the first "cardinal" marker. Immediately after crossing the Deck (basically the bridge over I-495) and before you reach St. Mary's Cemetery, turn right to head toward Maryland on the Woodrow Wilson Memorial Bridge.

1.6 Look closely on the ground and you'll see the border marker for Virginia and the District of Columbia. You are now in DC.

2.4 You've crossed the bridge and reached a small park area on the bridge deck dedicated to the history of Prince George's County, worth hanging out and reading some of the markers.

3.2 Continue straight and to the right on the gravel path toward National Harbor.

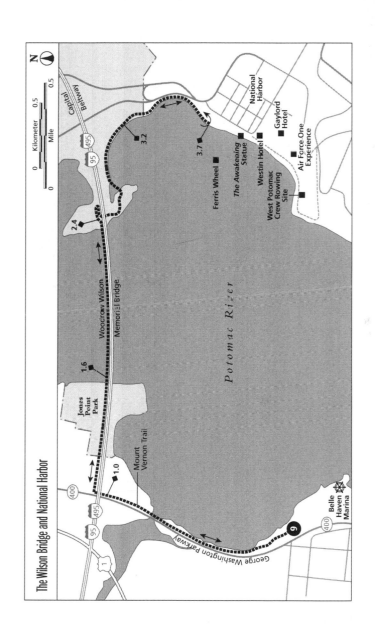

The Wilson Bridge and National Harbor

N

Capital Beltway

495
95

0.5   Kilometer   0   0.5
0   Mile   0.5

3.2

3.7

National Harbor

Gaylord Hotel

The Awakening Statue

Ferris Wheel

Westin Hotel

West Potomac Crew Rowing Site

Air Force One Experience

2.4

Woodrow Wilson Memorial Bridge

1.6

Jones Point Park

Mount Vernon Trail

Potomac River

1.0

400
495
95
1

9

George Washington Parkway

Belle Haven Marina

3.7 You've reached National Harbor. At this point you have various options: You can make a U-turn and return to Virginia along the same path, lock your bike and explore the area by foot, or, if you prefer, simply continue along the waterfront and up to National Plaza toward the Westin, where the bike path will continue along the waterfront toward the Air Force One Experience. The bike path will end on National Harbor Boulevard shortly after it circumvents Air Force One.

Ride Information

LOCAL EVENTS AND ATTRACTIONS
National Harbor: www.nationalharbor.com

BIKE SHOP
Spokes Etc., 1506 Belle View Blvd., Alexandria, VA 22307; (703) 765-8005; www.spokesetc.com

RESTAURANTS
There are a multitude of restaurants at National Harbor; visit www.nationalharbor.com/dine/ for a complete and up-to-date list of dining options.

10 The North Tract–Patuxent Wildlife Refuge

Both of the rides detailed here will take you through a tract of land that the Department of the Interior has designated to support and promote wildlife and has specifically set up for research, conservation, and wildlife education. The off-road loop is a perfect introduction to mountain biking and offers novice riders a chance to spin along wide old roads with very little elevation change through an area that has remained unchanged for quite some time. This is the perfect ride to bring your kids along. Meanwhile, the out-and-back road option gives riders a relatively safe road section to put in some miles, all while enjoying the isolation that the North Tract offers.

Start: Contact Station parking area. You must register at the Contact Station before entering and using the facilities.

Distance: 6.7-mile mountain bike loop/13.8-mile out-and-back road ride

Riding time: 1–1.5 hours for either ride

Best bike: Road, hybrid, or mountain bike

Terrain and surface type: Mostly flat, gravel and paved roads

Highlights: Wildlife viewing

Hazards: Stay alert for damage to pathways (potholes, washouts, big cracks).

Other considerations: Hunting is permitted on the refuge; check at the Control Station for information on hunter activity in the area.

Maps: USGS Laurel, MD

Getting there: From the Capital Beltway (I-495) take I-95 north toward Baltimore. Take exit 33A for MD 198 east. Continue on MD 198 for approximately 5 miles and turn right onto Bald

Eagle Drive. Continue on Bald
Eagle until you reach the Contact

Station. GPS: N39 04.663' /
W76 46.286'

The Ride

The Patuxent Research Refuge was established in 1936 by executive order of President Franklin Delano Roosevelt, making it the nation's first wildlife research station. The refuge extends for 12,000 acres across the Patuxent River Valley, between Baltimore and Washington. It is divided into three main tracts: North, Central, and South. The North Tract, where these rides take place, is open to the public for hunting, fishing, wildlife observation, hiking, bicycling, and horseback riding.

When you enter the North Tract, you are required to check in at the Contact Station. Why? Prior to the land being transferred to the Department of the Interior, the North Tract was once used by the US Army as a training facility, and although the area has been cleared of unexploded ordnance, managers don't want visitors to veer off the paths and accidentally find something they may have missed. And, the North Tract is an active research facility.

Patuxent, meaning "running over loose stones," was first inhabited by Native Americans and later settled by Europeans who built small farms and mills. Family cemeteries are all that remain of the early European settlers. Within the cemeteries—one of which we'll ride past—you may notice the name Snowden.

The Snowdens settled in this area in the late 1600s, when King Charles II granted Richard Snowden nearly 2,000 acres. Richard Snowden would eventually own more than 16,000 acres of land along the banks of the Patuxent. Birmingham

Manor, seat for the Snowden family, was a thriving plantation. Its current location is on the east side of the Baltimore-Washington Parkway, opposite the Laurel Airport.

In its prosperous days, the plantation had twenty-four tobacco barns all in a row. Unfortunately, a fire destroyed the Snowden home in 1891, and the surrounding buildings were demolished in 1953 to create the northbound lanes of the Baltimore-Washington Parkway. Rubble from the old home and two wells are still present next to the Snowden Cemetery. The Patuxent visitor center and the Patuxent Research Refuge website (www.fws.gov/refuge/patuxent) have additional information on the history of the North Tract, the Snowden family, and other families who were instrumental in shaping the state of Maryland.

Miles and Directions

Mountain bike gravel loop

0.0 Check in at the Contact Station and then ride your bike around the back of the building to access the Wildlife Loop. We'll begin measuring shortly before exiting the parking area by the small yard behind the Contact Station. Exit the parking area and turn right onto the Wildlife Loop. As the Wildlife Loop curves to the left, continue straight onto the gravel road. You can't miss it—this is Wild Turkey Way.

0.6 Continue to the right to remain on Wild Turkey Way. We'll return on the road to the left.

1.2 Bear right and follow the sign to enter Sweetgum Lane.

1.3 Turn right onto Whip-Poor-Will Way.

2.3 Continue following Whip-Poor-Will Way to the left.

2.9 Turn right onto Sweetgum Lane.

3.5 Turn left and continue on Sweetgum Lane.

4.1 Turn left at this intersection and then follow South Road to the right. (***Option:*** You can take Wild Turkey to the left for approximately 1 mile to the site of the Snowden Cemetery.)

5.6 Turn left onto Kingfisher.

6.1 Turn right onto Wild Turkey Way and backtrack to the Contact Station.

6.7 Continue straight onto the Wildlife Loop and then left back into the Contact Station.

Road bike out-and-back

0.0 Check in at the Contact Station and then ride your bike around the back of the building to access the Wildlife Loop. We'll begin measuring shortly before exiting the parking area by the small yard behind the Contact Station. Exit the parking area and turn right onto the Wildlife Loop. Continue following the pavement to the left. Do not enter the dirt road to the right. You'll stay on the paved road for the next 5 miles.

0.5 The wildlife viewing area is to your left.

5.1 Make a U-turn on the bridge and head back in the same direction you came.

10.2 The Contact Station is to your left. You can finish your ride here if you want, but we'll add a couple more miles to the ride.

12.0 Shortly after the entrance to the Lake Allen loop, make a U-turn and head back the same way you came to the Contact Station.

13.8 Turn right into the Contact Station parking area, and the loop is complete.

Ride Information

LOCAL EVENTS AND ATTRACTIONS

North Tract Programs: www.fws.gov/northeast/patuxent/ntedu.html

The North Tract—Patuxent Wildlife Refuge

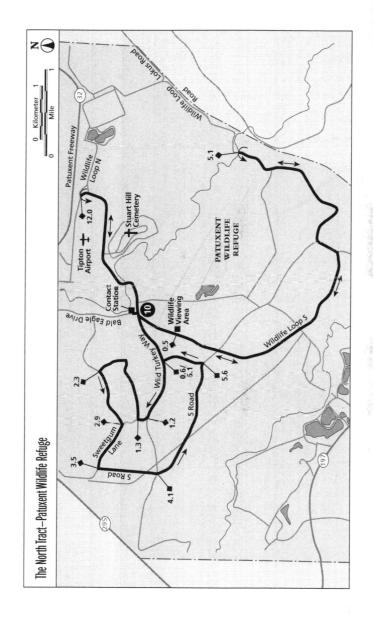

Laurel, Maryland: www.cityoflaurel.org/content/events

RESTAURANTS

Pasta Plus, 209 Gorman Ave., Laurel, MD 20707; (301) 498-5100; www.pastaplusrestaurant.com

Red Hot and Blue, 677 Main St., Laurel, MD 20707; (301) 953-1943; www.redhotandblue.com

RESTROOMS

Restrooms are available at the Contact Station.

11 South Germantown Bike Park

Unlike most rides detailed in this book, the South Germantown Bike Park is a destination. Chances are that once you arrive you'll just stay there and session the pump track and available jump lines. However, riders can easily access the Hoyles Mill Connector, Schaeffer Farms Trails, and the Diabase Trail from the South Germantown Bike Park. These and other trails in Montgomery County are documented in my other book, *Mountain Biking the Washington D.C./Baltimore Area.*

Start: Bike park
Distance: Varies
Riding time: Varies
Best bike: Mountain bike
Terrain and surface type: Unpaved jump lines and pump track
Highlights: Germantown Soccerplex
Hazards: Dirt jumping is an inherently dangerous activity; use caution and always wear a helmet.
Other considerations: The South Germantown Bike Park is centrally located. From it you can access over 50 miles of natural-surface trails. A 6-mile paved trail that winds in and around the park and its sports facilities is also accessible from this location. The paved trail is clearly marked and easy to follow.
Maps: USGS Kensington, MD
Getting there: From I-270 North exit onto MD 118 South, Germantown Road. Continue on MD 118 for 2.5 miles and turn right onto MD 117, Clopper Road, then make an immediate left onto Schaeffer Road. At the traffic circle, take the first exit onto Central Park Drive, which circles the complex. Take the first left and continue for approximately half a mile to the model boat play park. Park here. The bike park is on the opposite side of Central Park Drive, accessible via a short gravel road. GPS: N39 08.849' / W77 18.744'

The Ride

Had it not been for the extraordinary efforts of some, the South Germantown Bike Park would never have come to fruition. The now-popular cycling destination became a reality thanks to the efforts of several Mid-Atlantic Off-Road Enthusiasts (MORE) volunteers, in particular one, Todd Bauer. Around 2008, the popularity of small bike parks was surging. MORE was busy fundraising and planning the Rockburn Branch Skills Park, and former club member Larry Camp was working on a similar project in Chambersburg, Pennsylvania. Larry's ties to the Washington, DC, region were well established, and his close friendship with Todd prompted Todd to explore the possibility of doing something similar to the Pennsylvania project in Germantown.

After an initially frustrating and unsuccessful bid to make the project happen, Todd nearly gave up. In 2010, however, and thanks to efforts of Montgomery County's Bob Turnball in another unrelated project nearby, the stars realigned. Dirt from the construction of the Washington Nationals Miracle Field at South Germantown, a complex that provides individuals with disabilities the opportunity to play baseball, needed to be placed somewhere. Bob remembered Todd's bid to build the bike park and offered to help, but things needed to happen quickly. Basically, the county had the dirt and necessary equipment that Todd's vision needed, but not the plan.

Todd mobilized, and using trail reinvestment funds from the MoCo Epic, commissioned a plan from pump track guru Lee McCormack. Lee was able to deliver a comprehensive solution in record time, and Todd worked with the county to develop the landmark. The park was modest at first, consisting of just a pump track. Since then, MORE has continued to invest and expand the park to include progressive jumps, a pavilion, and additional wooden features for riders to hone their skills.

Since its inception the park has been the hub for MORE's signature event, the MoCo Epic, and is a central

YOU *WILL* RUN INTO TODD BAUER

I've known Todd for many years due to my involvement with the Mid-Atlantic Off-Road Enthusiasts (MORE) bike club. In that time he has become a trusted friend. Todd was not only instrumental in the development of the South Germantown Bike Park, but is also one of the driving forces that makes MORE's signature event, the MoCo Epic, happen every year. As if that's not enough, Todd has been a main contributor behind a unique project aimed at introducing young riders to the mountain biking community through MORE's sMORE's program.

Todd generally leads groups of kids along the trails in Montgomery County, showing them how to safely ride their bikes. "I simply love seeing the smiles on their faces when they clear an obstacle," he said. His rides are all about fun and provide kids with a low-stress environment so they can build their skills and confidence. That low-stress environment has proved so popular that even some adult beginners have joined in on the fun.

Todd is also a fixture at the South Germantown Bike Park, and if you ever ride the jump lines and pump track, chances are Todd's been around ensuring they are in great shape. If you see him, introduce yourself and say thanks for all the hard work. If you can, ask Todd how you too might lend a hand to ensure the dirt jumps remain smooth for all riders to enjoy.

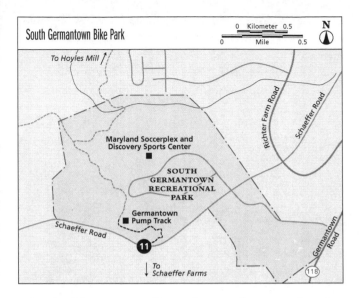

point for Montgomery County's expanding natural-surface trails.

Ride Information

LOCAL EVENTS AND ATTRACTIONS

Montgomery County's official website with local information: www.montgomerycountymd.gov

BIKE SHOPS

Germantown Cycles, 12619-L Wisteria Dr., Germantown, MD 20874; (240) 404-0695; www.germantowncycles.com

RESTAURANTS

Picca Chicken, 13000 Middlebrook Rd., Germantown, MD 20874; (301) 540-6500; www.picca.com

Dogfish Head Alehouse, 800 W. Diamond Ave., Gaithersburg, MD 20878; (301) 963-4847; https://dogfishalehouse.com

RESTROOMS
Available throughout the park

12 Rockburn Branch Park and Skills Park

Rockburn Branch Park, home to the award-winning Rockburn Branch Skills Park, is an excellent place to introduce people to mountain biking. Its rolling trails give novice to intermediate cyclists a chance to focus on developing their skills. If you want to pack on the miles, you should definitely combine Rockburn's picturesque trails with the more advanced paths of Patapsco's Avalon area.

Start: The Rockburn trails can be accessed from various locations; I recommend parking in the parking area beyond field #3. From there you can easily access the dirt road that leads up to the skills park, or the trailhead that leads into the majority of the natural-surface trails on the south side of the park.

Distance: Varies depending on trails ridden (there are 6.6 miles of natural-surface trails at Rockburn)

Riding time: Varies depending on trails ridden and skill level

Best bike: Mountain bike

Terrain and surface type: Mostly doubletrack, some singletrack, and several sections of asphalt, mostly on the park's north and west sides. The skills area includes dirt jumps, rock gardens, and wood features.

Highlights: Award-winning skills park

Hazards: Other riders; use caution on the skills area.

Other considerations: Please don't ride when wet. Also, Rockburn is bustling with other activity during the spring and summer months; parking areas and roads can have lots of traffic.

Maps: USGS Savage, MD

Getting there: Take I-95 north to exit 43B and merge onto MD 100 West toward Ellicott City. Take exit 4 for MD 103 East. Turn right at the traffic circle to continue on MD 103/Meadowbridge Road. Continue for approximately 1.5

miles and turn right onto Ilchester Road, then turn right onto Landing Road. The park entrance will be approximately 1.3 miles farther, on your right. Once you enter the park, simply follow the road until it ends at a small traffic circle beyond field #3. Shortly before you reach the traffic circle, you will notice a dirt road to the right. This is the access point to the Rockburn Branch Skills Park. GPS: N39 13.226' / W76 45.667'

The Ride

One of the most popular riding destinations in the Washington, DC/Baltimore area is Patapsco Valley State Park. But not many people know that adjacent to Patapsco is Rockburn Branch Regional Park, part of Howard County's 7,000 acre scenic park system. This vibrant parcel of parkland is managed by Howard County and has more than 6 miles of dirt trails on which to ride and a riding skills park (www.rockburn skillspark.com), which includes an extremely popular jump line and pump track.

Although not nearly as technical or hilly as the trails in Patapsco, Rockburn Branch offers a series of well-marked trails that will delight any mountain bike lover. The park, located in northern Howard County, is not only a trail playground but also a popular destination for many sports enthusiasts. There are more than eight softball and baseball fields, numerous basketball courts, several soccer and football fields, four tennis courts, and several children's play areas. In addition, during the spring and summer months, the park has a snack and concession stand offering freshly cooked burgers and hot dogs. Rockburn is also a popular picnic destination for those less interested in adrenaline and more in pleasing the palate.

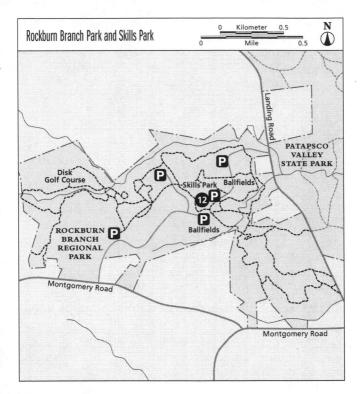

Rockburn Branch Park and Skills Park

0 Kilometer 0.5

0 Mile 0.5

N

Landing Road

PATAPSCO VALLEY STATE PARK

Disk Golf Course

Skills Park

Ballfields

ROCKBURN BRANCH REGIONAL PARK

Ballfields

Montgomery Road

Montgomery Road

Miles and Directions

Rockburn Branch is compact, and the trails are well marked and easy to follow. For that reason, I'm only providing you with a starting point and general guidance on where to head. Park at the far end of the parking area beyond field #3 and just past the dirt road that leads up to the skills park (you can also park by the skills park along the dirt road). From there you can access both the skills park (up along the dirt road to the right) and the trailhead that will give you access to the park's natural-surface trails (along the small traffic circle).

You can also access the trails at Patapsco's Avalon from here by following the yellow trail under the power lines toward Landing Road and the trailhead (Morning Choice Trail) into Patapsco Valley State Park. There are more than 20 miles of great riding in this portion of Patapsco, with access to many more.

Ride Information

LOCAL INFORMATION
Howard County, Maryland: www.visithowardcounty.com

RESTAURANTS
There is an abundance of restaurants in Columbia and Ellicott City, both within proximity of Rockburn Branch Park. Two of my local favorites are:

Frisco Taphouse, 6695 Dobbin Rd., Ste. G, Columbia, MD 21045; (410) 312-4907; www.friscotaphouse.com

Modern Market Eatery, 6181 Old Dobbin Ln., Ste. 200, Columbia, MD 21045; (443) 583-3337; https://modern market.com

13 The Seneca Ridge Trail

The Seneca Ridge Trail (SRT) is one of the region's most impressive trails in the vast catalog of off-road riding destinations. The 7-mile ribbon of singletrack connects Schaffer's white loop with the Seneca Creek Park System.

Start: Black Rock Mill parking area. The trail can also be accessed from Schaeffer Farms via the Schaeffer SRT Connector.
Distance: 11.6 miles out and back
Riding time: 1.5–3 hours
Best bike: Mountain bike
Terrain and surface type: Rolling singletrack
Highlights: Points of interest along the way
Hazards: Use caution at all road crossings.
Other considerations: Please don't ride these trails after heavy rain or when wet and muddy.
Maps: USGS Germantown and Seneca, MD

Getting there: From I-270, take exit 15 for MD 118 South toward Germantown. Continue on MD 118 for 3.6 miles and turn right onto Black Rock Road. Drive approximately 2 miles; the trailhead is adjacent to the Black Rock Mill, on the right. There is limited parking in and around the mill. GPS: N39 07.623' / W77 18.863'

An alternate starting point is the Schaeffer Farms parking area. From there you can ride the white trail to the Seneca Ridge Trail (SRT) Connector and then pick up the Seneca Ridge Trail (SRT).

The Ride

Back in the mid-1990s I had the pleasure of heading out with local advocacy guru David Scull on a flagging mission to Schaeffer Farms. Much of the wooded land around the farms eventually became the Schaeffer Farms mountain bike trail system. Little did we know how far those first steps would take the mountain bike community and how important that park would become in the development of off-road cycling in the region.

Today there are more than 18 miles of singletrack trails in that park alone. And, thanks to the efforts of another advocacy guru, Dave Magill, there is a signature strip of trail extending from Schaeffer Farms to the trails at Clopper Lake, the Seneca Ridge Trail (SRT).

The genesis of the SRT harkens to the time when the Schaeffer Farms trails were first being built. The hiker-only Seneca Greenway Trail was also under construction, and unfortunately it was unfeasible to build a second multiuse trail alongside it, simply because the area along Seneca Creek was too narrow and could not support two trails. Further-more, it was impossible to build a throughway because of the existence of a shooting range along the creek.

That all changed, however, when in 2008 the lease for the shooting range expired, and the Maryland Department of Natural Resources (DNR) decided not to renew it. That cre-ated the opportunity for the SRT to be built. Mid-Atlantic Off-Road Enthusiasts (MORE) developed a proposal for DNR in which they outlined how to provide all the neces-sary funds and labor to build the new multiuse trail.

In September 2011, the group completed the 6.25 miles of trail that connected the Schaeffer Farms white loop with Seneca Creek State Park, just in time for its annual fall picnic. The second trail, the Seneca Bluffs Trail, was completed in time for the 2012 MoCo Epic.

The SRT has quickly become one of my favorite single-track rides in the region. The flow of the trail is fantastic and was built with the cross-country rider in mind. It uses the contours almost perfectly and is an absolute joy to ride. If you are a beginner to intermediate rider you'll love it, because it caters to your abilities. If you are an advanced rider you'll simply adore it, because it will give you an opportunity to find a rhythm you seldom can on other regional trails.

Miles and Directions

0.0 Start from the trailhead at Black Rock Road. The SRT is immediately across the street from the mill parking area.

0.6 Continue straight through the intersection. This is the first of several neighborhood connectors. As you continue on the SRT, you will encounter several more of these branch trails. From trail wear it is quite obvious which is the SRT and which are simply neighborhood connectors.

1.9 Cross Germantown Road (MD 118). Use caution.

2.9 Continue straight through the intersection.

3.9 Stay to the left at the intersection.

4.1 Stay left past two intersections.

5.8 You've reached the end of the SRT. Turn around and head back along the same path. (*Option:* Alternatively, you can cross Riffle Ford Road and make your way into Seneca Creek State Park.)

11.6 Arrive back at the trailhead.

Ride Information

LOCAL EVENTS AND ATTRACTIONS
Montgomery County's official website with local information: www.montgomerycountymd.gov

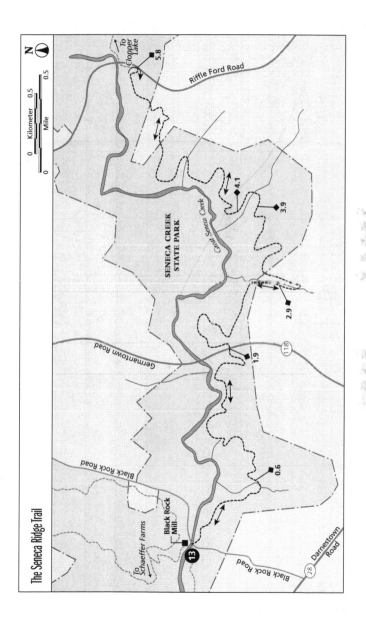

The Seneca Ridge Trail

BIKE SHOPS
Germantown Cycles, 12619-L Wisteria Dr., Germantown, MD 20874; (240) 404-0695; www.germantowncycles.com

RESTAURANTS
Picca Chicken, 13000 Middlebrook Rd., Germantown, MD 20874; (301) 540-6500; www.picca.com

Dogfish Head Alehouse, 800 W. Diamond Ave., Gaithersburg, MD 20878; (301) 963-4847; https://dogfishalehouse.com

14 Burke Lake and Mercer Lake

If there was ever a "family" ride, the Burke Lake Loop is it. The loop takes riders on a mostly flat path along flower gardens. You'll enjoy the panoramic vistas of Burke Lake, a man-made body of water that also serves as one of the busiest fishing reservoirs in the metro Washington, DC, area.

Start: All options start from the South Run Trails trailhead adjacent to the South Run Recreation Center Field House

Distance: Burke Lake Loop, 7.4 miles; Mercer Lake Loop, 4.1 miles; both loops, 11.3 miles

Riding time: 45 minutes–2 hours depending on route chosen

Best bike: Hybrid, mountain, or cyclo-cross bike; kids' bikes will do fine here.

Terrain and surface type: Mostly flat, paved paths and doubletrack dirt trails

Highlights: Waterfowl. Occasional bald eagles and panoramic views of Burke Lake

Hazards: Other trail users

Other considerations: Pathways can get crowded on summer weekends; watch for errant riders, hikers, and users with headphones.

Maps: USGS Fairfax and Occoquan, VA

Getting there: From the Capital Beltway (I-495), take exit 54 for Braddock Road West. Continue on Braddock Road for approximately 1.5 miles and turn left onto Burke Lake Road. In approximately 2.5 miles turn left onto Lee Chapel Road (VA 643) and continue for 2 miles to the Fairfax County Parkway. Turn left onto the parkway and then right onto Preservation Road. Follow the road into South Run Park until it ends in a small gravel lot behind the South Run Recreation Center Field House. GPS: N38 44.862' / W77 16.555'

The Ride

After World War II, the aviation industry around the country was thriving. One particular area to benefit from this boom was the Washington, DC, area. The town of Burke and the area where Burke Lake currently sits were selected for a much-needed second regional airport. The proposed location of the new international airport would occupy nearly 4,500 acres and displace hundreds of families. According to a June 14, 1951, article in the *Evening Star*, the proposed airport would be completed by 1955 and would "dwarf both Washington and Baltimore's Friendship terminals."

Understandably, Burke residents opposed the proposal, and thanks to some great leadership, the location was reconsidered. and in 1958 the planned facility was built to the west in the town of Willard, present-day Chantilly. That airport, as we know it today, is Washington Dulles.

Fairfax County acquired the land originally set aside for the airport project in 1959 and opted to follow the suggestions of its citizens to create a recreational area, including a public fishing lake. Nearly 2,000 people attended the facility's opening ceremonies on May 25, 1963. Today the 218-acre Burke Lake is surrounded by nearly 900 acres of wooded parkland, making it one of the county's largest lake parks. It is a peaceful place to spend time and go for a bike ride on the lake's perimeter trail. From the trail you can catch a glimpse of an elusive bald eagle or one of the many waterfowl that call the lake home.

The lake is extremely popular, primarily because of its family-oriented attractions, including camping, several picnic areas, a playground, and a Frisbee golf course. The park also operates a miniature railroad that has been running for over forty years. It's not uncommon to see parents who as kids rode the train themselves enjoying it with their children. The second miniature replica of the Central Pacific's steam engine chugs around the 1.75 miles of track in about 10 minutes. There is also an old-fashioned carousel. And, if you tire of everything the park has to offer, you can take a quick ride over Ox Road to the adjacent driving ranges and golf courses, which include a school for aspiring golfers of all ages, or farther south to the Lorton Arts Center, where local artists have studios open to the public.

Miles and Directions

You can do either one of the recommended loops or combine both for a longer ride.

Both rides

0.0 Start from the gravel lot at the far end of the South Run Recreation Center by the field house. The South Run Trail entrance is clearly marked with a trail map kiosk.

0.2 Turn left toward Mercer Lake or right toward Burke Lake.

Mercer Lake

0.3 Turn left and away from the paved trail and onto the gravel trail.

0.6 Continue following the gravel path to the left.

0.7 Cross the cul-de-sac onto the gravel path directly opposite on the other side.

1.1 Turn left and head up the short hill, then turn right onto the paved path at the top.

1.8 Go through the trail barrier and continue straight over the dam. (**Note**: The left fork takes you through the South Run Stream Valley Park and ends within close distance of the

Cross County Trail). After crossing the dam, continue following the main trail to the right to stay along the perimeter of the lake. You'll pass several neighborhood "feeder" trails.

3.7 Turn right at this T intersection and head over the bridge. Continue following the trail to the left toward the starting point of the loop.

3.9 If you want to continue to Burke Lake, turn left at this intersection and follow the directions below. A right turn will take you back to the parking area and your vehicle.

4.1 You're back at the starting point.

Burke Lake

1.4 You've reached the Burke Lake Loop. At this point, you can go either direction; the trail is easy and follows the perimeter of the lake. If you ride in a counterclockwise direction, just stay to the left at pretty much all intersections. If you ride clockwise, which is the direction we will be heading, stay to the right. As you reach the parking areas, there are clear signs that point you in the right direction to stay on the "Park Trail."

2.7 See signs of the miniature railroad tracks.

3.2 Continue following the trail to the right as it parallels Burke Lake Road and immediately heads back into the woods to the right.

6.0 Turn left and backtrack toward the start.

7.2 Veer left at the intersection and continue up to the parking area.

7.4 Finish the loop.

Ride Information

LOCAL EVENTS AND ATTRACTIONS

Burke Lake Park offers fishing, boating, and a great Frisbee golf course. Farther north is the **Fairfax Station**

Burke Lake and Mercer Lake

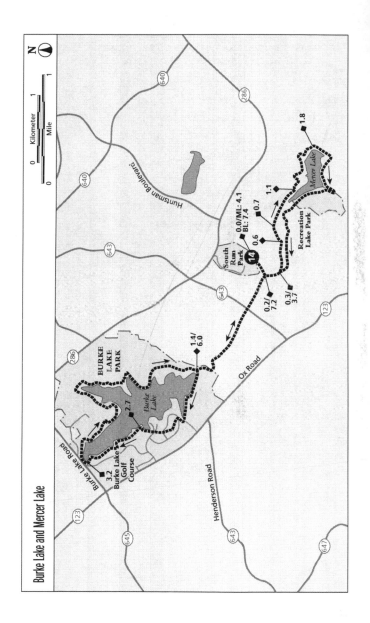

Railroad Museum: https://fairfax-station.org. **Go Ape Zipline & Treetop Adventures** is just southeast: www.goape.com.

RESTAURANTS
Squisito Pizza and Pasta, 8971 Ox Rd. #245, Lorton, VA 22079; (703) 646-5248; www.squisitopizzaandpasta.com

15 Laurel Hill

The ride through the hills and meadows of Laurel Hill will take you through a parcel of land that was once home to a Revolutionary War hero and thousands of reformatory inmates.

Start: Equestrian parking area on Dairy Road
Distance: 3.6-mile figure-eight loop (there are nearly 12 miles of trails at Laurel Hill)
Riding time: 0.5–1 hour
Best bike: Mountain bike
Terrain and surface type: Mostly doubletrack and singletrack trails
Highlights: Old penitentiary buildings
Hazards: Loose gravel trails can be difficult for beginners.
Other considerations: Ticks are abundant during the spring and summer.
Maps: USGS Occoquan and Fort Belvoir, VA

Getting there: Laurel Hill is in Lorton, Virginia, approximately 20 miles south of Washington, DC. From I-95 take the Lorton Road exit. Head west at the bottom of the ramp (a right turn whether coming north- or southbound on I-95). After approximately 1 mile turn left onto Furnace Road and then immediately right onto Dairy Road. The parking area is approximately 0.25 mile to your right. Use caution as you drive. Use caution as you drive in; look for riders and other trail users. GPS: N38 42.063' / W77 14.761'

The Ride

Named after the original hometown of one of the area's first settlers, Joseph Plaskett, Lorton has a colorful history. And Laurel Hill, the geographic area where this ride takes place, is no different.

The area had been home to the Powhatan people, a confederation of tribes that farmed and hunted the lands of the coastal plains and tidewater region. Like in so many regions in the East, it didn't take long for the Native Americans to be displaced by the arriving settlers. Yet it really wasn't until Joseph Plaskett added a post office in the mid-1800s to his popular country store that Lorton was finally placed on the map.

Roughly around the same time that Lorton gained postal recognition, another prominent American settled in the area. William Lindsay, a major in one of Virginia's militias during the Revolutionary War and a presumed aide to George Washington himself, built a home for his family on a hilltop overlooking his 1,000-acre plantation and named it Laurel Hill after what is believed to have been the original Lindsay family estate in Ireland. Lindsay spent his last decade alongside his wife and sixteen children at Laurel Hill, and upon his death in 1792 was buried at the estate, where his grave remains visible to this day.

The area remained in the shadows until the early twentieth century, when then-president Theodore Roosevelt commissioned the building of a penitentiary for the District of Columbia in the meadows of Laurel Hill. The prison's dwindling popularity, changing attitudes, and the sprawl of the late twentieth century toward the Virginia suburbs forced its closure and ultimate transfer to Fairfax County by the beginning of the twenty-first century.

By November 2001, with the transfer of the last of the prisoners from the penitentiary complete, the Lorton prison was officially closed and thus began the renovation of the Lorton facilities.

Today the area is most commonly referred to as Laurel Hill to honor the legacy of William Lindsay and to preserve its historical significance.

Over the past two decades, the facilities have seen a dramatic change. Several of the old penitentiary buildings have been restored and now house a thriving community of artists and craftspeople that host cultural and community events. An

YOU MAY RUN INTO MIKE APPLEGATE

If you ride the Laurel Hill trails more than once, chances are you will run into Mike Applegate. Mike, a retired Marine, has devoted his off time to volunteering for MORE and Fairfax County and is largely responsible for ensuring the trails in this regional Fairfax County destination are rideable, safe, and accessible for all mountain bikers to enjoy all the time. Shortly after the trails were built, they were notoriously overgrown and rife with ticks. For that reason many riders avoided them in the spring and summer months. But since Mike took over maintenance duties, the field trails are kept meticulously mowed and trimmed. Puddles are quickly nicked and filled, and downed trees are rapidly removed from the corridor.

"I simply enjoy being outside," Mike told me during a recent encounter. "Having something to do outside during beautiful days helps me enjoy my retirement; it's especially gratifying to see so many people enjoy the trails and meeting them as they ride by." If you encounter Mike on the trail, take a minute to stop and say hi, and thank him for keeping this regional destination in such great shape for everyone to enjoy.

eighteen-hole golf course is up and running, and an extensive system of trails has been built and is now open for the enjoyment of the community.

Miles and Directions

Laurel Hill is composed of multiple intersecting loops and one point-to-point trail, Giles Run. There are a myriad of options when riding this system. The loop below represents a small portion of that system. As you become more comfortable on your bike, I recommend you explore more of the trails in this destination.

0.0   Ride away from the parking area in the direction you drove in; the trail crosses Dairy Road. Turn right to access the trail. The trail will immediately fork; stay to the left to access the Pasture Loop.

0.4   Continue to the right. A left turn will take you up to Furnace Road and the access point for the Apple Orchard loop. The Apple Orchard Loop can add an additional 1.6 miles to your ride.

0.6   Continue to the right past the next two intersections to remain on the Pasture Loop. The two trails to the left are the entry and exit points to the 0.5-mile Power Station Loop.

0.9   Continue following the trail straight. You are now on the Dairy Barn Loop. A sharp right will take you back to the starting point of the ride (approximately 0.1 mile).

1.9   Reach Dairy Road. The trail continues on the opposite side. A right turn will take you back to the starting point (approximately 0.2 mile).

2.2   The parking area is to your right. Had enough? Turn right to end the ride, or continue to the left on the Workhouse Trail.

2.7   Continue to the left to remain on the Workhouse Trail. A right turn will take you to the Cross County Trail (CCT).

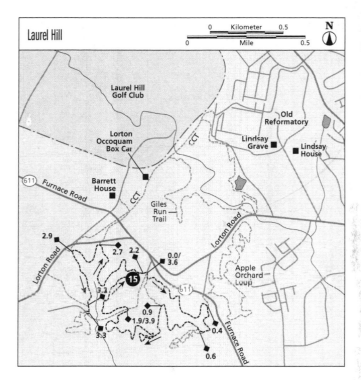

2.9 Continue to the left at this intersection. A right will take you to the CCT. The next section is super fun!

3.2 Turn left at this intersection to head back down toward Dairy Road. Following the trail to the right will take you to the CCT.

3.3 Reach the bottom of Dairy Road. Make a left to head back up the hill toward the parking area. A right turn will take you to the entrance of the 0.5-mile Slaughterhouse Trail.

3.4 Continue past this intersection, which we passed a little while ago (mile 1.9).

3.6 The loop is complete.

Ride Information

LOCAL EVENTS AND ATTRACTIONS

Workhouse Arts Center: www.lortonarts.org/calendar.php

Town of Occoquan: occoquanva.gov

Lorton, Virginia: www.virginia.org/cities/lorton

BIKE SHOPS

The Bike Lane, 8416 Old Keene Mill Rd., Springfield, VA 22151; (703) 440-8701; www.thebikelane.com

Olde Towne Bicycles, 14519 Potomac Mills Rd., Woodbridge, VA 22192; (703) 491-5700; www.oldetownebicycles .com

RESTAURANTS

Squisito Pizza and Pasta, 8971 Ox Rd. #245, Lorton, VA 22079; (703) 646-5248; www.squisitopizzaandpasta.com

Glory Days Grill, 9459 Lorton Market St., Lorton, VA 22079; (703) 372-1770; www.glorydaysgrill.com

Vinny's Italian Grill, 7730 Gunston Plaza, Lorton, VA 22079; (703) 339-7447; www.vinnysitaliangrill.net

16 **Wakefield Park**

Wakefield Park is quite possibly one of the most popular, if not the most popular, mountain bike destinations in the metro Washington, DC, area. Its close proximity to the Capital Beltway makes it a popular destination for all the northern Virginia suburbanites who live and/or work inside or near the Beltway.

Start: Audrey Moore RECenter parking area
Distance: 5.5-mile loop
Riding time: About 1 hour
Best bike: Mountain bike
Terrain and surface type: Dirt singletrack trails
Highlights: The power line berms
Hazards: Small bridges and other trail obstacles
Other considerations: Please don't ride Wakefield after periods of heavy rain.
Maps: USGS Annandale, VA

Getting there: The park is less than 0.5 mile from the Capital Beltway off Braddock Road in northern Virginia. From I-495 exit west on exit 54A, Braddock Road, and turn right in less than 2 miles into Wakefield. Drive straight for approximately 0.5 mile and then turn left where the tarmac ends into the main Audrey Moore RECenter parking area. GPS: N38 49.066' / W77 13.406'

The Ride

The trails at Wakefield have been through a drastic transformation over the past decades. The early popularity of mountain biking in the mid-1990s and into the 2000s brought a tremendous number of riders into the park. Unfortunately, the original power line and wooded trails that existed within its boundaries were not designed for off-road cycling and therefore suffered considerably with the number of riders that used them on a daily basis. Park managers and the Mid-Atlantic Off-Road Enthusiasts (MORE) recognized the problem and took action to improve and preserve the network of trails.

With the help of an International Mountain Biking Association (IMBA) trail crew, the muscle of local volunteers, and the support of Fairfax County government, regional riders set out to improve the trails of this Beltway destination. Thanks to the efforts and dedication of those biking advocates, today the park in Wakefield houses more than 6 miles of sustainable, enjoyable, and challenging trails, all within 0.5 mile of the Capital Beltway.

This ride will take you through those renovated trails. While challenging, Wakefield can be easily conquered by beginner riders and enjoyed by accomplished dirt lovers alike.

Miles and Directions

Wakefield Park is compact and the trails are relatively easy to follow. They are framed by the Beltway on one side and Accotink Creek on the other. For that reason, I'm only providing you with a starting point and general guidance on where to go. My advice is just to go out and explore all the trails around the power lines to find the loop that you like best. Park in the main Audrey Moore RECenter parking area and ride north on the gravel road that parallels I-495. Once you reach the power substation, the gravel will end and the trails will begin. Follow either fork to the power lines; from there the trails are easy to find. Once you ride them, you'll begin to get a sense for the best lines.

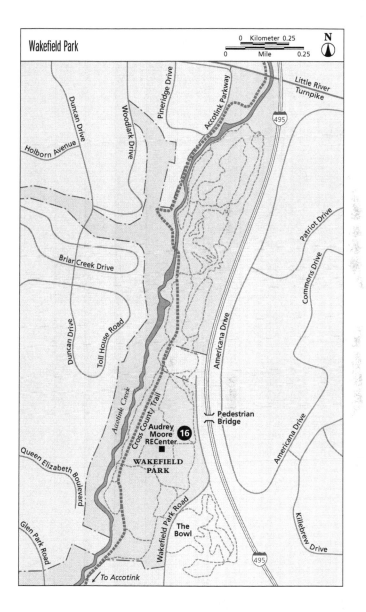

Wakefield Park

If you are looking for an "easier" ride, stick to the trails along the creek, since these tend to be flat with little elevation change. If you are looking for a challenge, I suggest you venture out into The Bowl, a short network of trails with lots of punchy climbs.

Ride Information

Fairfax County Convention and Visitors Bureau: (800) 7FAIRFAX; www.visitfairfax.org

LOCAL EVENTS AND ATTRACTIONS
Wakefield Farmers' Market: Wednesdays, 2–6 p.m., May 2–October 31

Mountain bike races are conducted throughout the summer, including the Wednesdays at Wakefield (W@W) Mountain Bike race series (www.wednesdaysatwakefield .com).

Trail-running races are conducted within Wakefield Park as a part of the Backyard Burn race series coordinated by EX2 Adventures (www.ex2adventures.com) in the spring and fall.

BIKE SHOPS
Bicycle Pro Shop, 5230-A Port Royal Rd., Springfield, VA 22151; (571) 297-4227

The Bike Lane, 8416 Old Keene Mill Rd., Springfield, VA, 22151; (703) 440-8701, www.thebikelane.com

RESTAURANTS
Kilroy's, 5250-A Port Royal Rd., Springfield, VA 22151; (703) 321-7733, www.kilroys.com

17 Conway Robinson State Forest

Although short, the ride will certainly be a pleasing one. It has quickly become a favorite destination for my daughter and me to visit. The relatively flat trails and smooth surface make it a perfect destination for novice to intermediate riders.

Start: Conway Robinson parking area

Distance: 3.3-mile loop; additional if you ride the internal trails

Riding time: Up to 1 hour

Best bike: Mountain bike

Terrain and surface type: Doubletrack and singletrack trails

Highlights: Pine and old-growth hardwood stands; wildlife and wildflower sanctuary.

Hazards: Hikers, equestrians, and hunters in season

Other considerations: Conway Robinson tends to hold water

after periods of rain, especially some of the internal trails. Don't ride when wet and muddy.

Maps: USGS Gainsville, VA

Getting there: Follow Route I-66W to exit 43B, US 29 N. Follow 29 North and make an immediate left on University Boulevard into the park's parking area. The trailhead is to the left of the main picnic area (as you face it). GPS: N44 58.235' / W93 16.988'

The Ride

Conway Robinson State Forest is adjacent to the Manassas National Battlefield. Situated in Prince William County and near the junction of the Alexandria and Manassas Gap Railroads, it served as a key link to the South. Confederate generals recognized the geographic significance of the area and stationed their troops to protect and maintain possession of the Manassas railroad junction, a key access point to the South's capital, Richmond, Virginia.

Only a few months had passed since the start of the Civil War when Northern citizens began clamoring for an advance on Richmond. Yielding to pressure, Brigadier General Irvin McDowell led his inexperienced army across Bull Run and through much of the area where Conway Robinson State Forest is today, toward Manassas. Their aim was to capture Manassas Junction.

The Southern army met the "surprise" attack planned by the North with conviction on July 21, 1861. Led by a relatively unknown officer from the Virginia Military Institute (VMI), Thomas Jackson, the Southern forces held their ground and drove the Northern forces back toward Washington. It was in that first battle that Jackson earned his nickname, "Stonewall." Jackson's brigade suffered considerable casualties that day, but they stopped the Union's assault and helped drive it back. It was another officer in the Southern forces, Brigadier General Barnard Elliott Bee Jr., who uttered the words that earned him and his brigade their nickname: "Look at Jackson standing there like a stone wall." It was also the first time that Union soldiers heard the "Rebel yell." It was Jackson who instructed his troops to "yell like furies" when they advanced and charged the enemy.

Both the South and North suffered great casualties in the First Manassas, and both armies came to the realization that the war would be longer, more arduous, and more brutal than anyone had anticipated.

Today, Conway Robinson State Forest offers us a glimpse into the past. Acquired by the state in 1938, Conway Robinson State Forest is an urban oasis dedicated to the preservation of the natural woodland within it. Named after Conway

Robinson, a prominent nineteenth-century Virginian, the 444-acre parcel remains one of the largest undeveloped parcels of land amid the suburban jungle of northern Virginia. Hikers, cyclists, equestrians, and hunters can now enjoy an environment that has been carefully managed through passive silviculture techniques—the practice of controlling the growth, composition, and quality of forests.

Miles and Directions

We will ride the Conway trails in a clockwise loop. Although Conway has many intersecting trails, these tend to be very muddy, even long after rain has passed.

0.0 The trailhead is to the left of the pavilion as you look at it from the parking area. The trail is blazed blue. Immediately upon entering the trail, stay to the left.

0.2 Cross the doubletrack to stay on the blue trail.

0.5 Stay to the right. The left branch is a neighborhood connector.

0.7 Stay to the left to continue to follow the blue loop.

0.8 Turn left onto the orange trail. The orange trail is the most technically difficult portion of this ride. You can bypass it and continue straight on the blue trail if you want.

1.5 Reach the blue loop again. Turn left to continue on the blue loop; right will simply take you back to the entry to the orange trail.

1.6 Continue following the blue trail as it curves to the left.

1.9 Turn left to continue following the blue blazes under the pines.

2.2 Turn right on the doubletrack. When I documented this ride, the forest service had done a controlled burn on the woods to the left.

2.5 Turn right to continue on the blue trail and the singletrack. Straight ahead will take you to US 29 (Lee Highway).

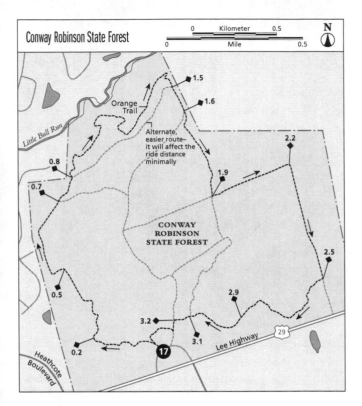

2.9 Go over the bridge.

3.1 Stay to the left to stay on the blue trail. The red trail to the right is notoriously muddy and best avoided.

3.2 Turn left on the yellow trail. This doubletrack will lead you back to the parking area. Immediately turn right to hop on the blue trail and ride behind the picnic pavilion. At the T intersection, turn left on the blue to complete the ride, or turn right and do the whole loop again.

3.3 The loop is complete.

Ride Information

The city of Manassas is rich in history, and there is a lot to do in the area year-round. Check out www.visitmanassas.org for regional attractions and the City of Manassas website, www.manassascity.org, for additional information.

LOCAL EVENTS AND ATTRACTIONS
Manassas National Battlefield Park: www.nps.gov/mana/index.htm

BIKE SHOPS
Bull Run Bicycles, 10458 Dumfries Rd., Manassas, VA 20110; (703) 335-6131; www.bullrunbicycles.com

A-1 Manassas Cycling, 7705 Sudley Rd., Manassas, VA 20109; (703) 361-6101; www.a1cycling.com

RESTAURANTS
Jimbo's Grill, 7901 Heritage Village Plaza, Gainesville, VA 20155; (571) 248-0752; www.jimbosgrill.com

Okra's Cajun Creole Restaurant, 9110 Center St., Manassas, VA 20110; (703) 330-2729; https://okras.com

2 Silos Brewing Co., 9925 Discovery Blvd., Manassa, VA 20109; (703) 420-2264; https://2silosbrewing.com

18 The Meadowood Recreation Area

This ride will take you through mature hardwood forests in the Mason Neck Peninsula.

Start: Gunston Road parking lot
Distance: 3.5- to 7-mile loop
Riding time: 0.5–1.5 hours depending on trails chosen
Best bike: Mountain bike
Terrain and surface type: Mostly singletrack with man-made features
Highlights: The big berm, elevated boardwalks
Hazards: Other trail users; Meadowood can be very busy on a nice day.
Other considerations: Meadowood is susceptible to damage after heavy rain; do not ride the trails when wet or muddy.

Maps: USGS Fort Belvoir, VA
Getting there: Take the Capital Beltway, I-495, toward northern Virginia and follow the signs for I-95 South. Take exit 163 for VA 642 toward Lorton and turn left onto Lorton Road. Follow Lorton Road for approximately 0.5 mile and turn right onto Lorton Market Street. Lorton Market Street will become Gunston Cove Road and then Gunston Road once you cross US 1. The parking area will be approximately 1 mile to your right immediately after Gunston Elementary School. GPS: N38 40.983' / W77 12.546'

The Ride

In the short time since the Meadowood biking trails were opened for riding, they have become one of the region's most popular mountain bike destinations. The nearly 800 acres of meadows, ponds, and hardwood forests where the trails currently lie were transferred in a land swap between Pulte Home Builders, Fairfax County, and the federal government in 2001. In late October of the same year, the land was assigned to the Bureau of Land Management (BLM), which currently manages it to ensure an open space for recreation and environmental education.

Before the land was transferred to the BLM, it had been a working farm that included a series of trails in varying states of disrepair. Once BLM took over the day-to-day management of the location, they fixed some immediate problems and developed an activity plan in which they outlined their vision for the area and identified the potential use scenarios. These included hiking, fishing, horseback riding, and cycling (mountain biking).

Meadowood is physically divided into two distinct areas by Belmont Boulevard. The east side of the system, closest to the Meadowood Field Station and adjacent to the existing horse boarding stables, is primarily an equestrian destination; bikes are not allowed there. The west side had remained undeveloped, and since mountain biking would be one of the allowed activities, BLM worked with then International Mountain Biking Association (IMBA) representative and trail specialist Dan Hudson to lay out a potential biking and hiking loop.

In 2009 the BLM, using American Recovery and Reinvestment Act (ARRA) funds, hired two staff members, Doug Vinson and David Lyster, with trail building experience to oversee the recommendations made by Dan Hudson and IMBA. After a period of additional planning, Vinson and Lyster began building the South Branch loop in early 2011. By January 2012, they had completed the loop detailed here. Phase 2 of the Meadowood project added three additional directional trails, including an advanced line, Boss Trail; a jump line, Yard Sale; and a tight singletrack option, Stinger. Riders can easily incorporate any or all of these internal options to lengthen their outings.

Miles and Directions

We'll be riding the loop counterclockwise, but this trail can be ridden in either direction. To add additional distance, incorporate one or all of the internal trails. The South Branch loop is very easy to follow. If this is your first time, I recommend you do one full loop of the South Branch Trail and then venture into the internal lines.

0.0 Drop into the trail and make an immediate right to access the South Branch loop.

0.9 The exit of the directional Boss Trail is to the left. Continue straight.

1.0 Continue following the trail to the left; the right spur will take you to the alternate, and smaller, Old Colchester Road parking area.

1.2 The entrance to the intermediate/advanced Boss Trail is to the left. Continue straight. Boss Trail is approximately 0.75 mile long; making a left to ride it and returning to this spot on the loop trail will add about a mile to your ride.

1.4 Continue straight through this intersection.

1.5 Continue to the left. You'll ride through a series of three additional trail junction points; remain left at all of them and follow the clearly marked South Branch Trail.

1.8 You've reached the boardwalk. Cross it and continue straight and up on the trail.

1.9 The exit of the directional Yard Sale Trail is to the left. Continue straight.

2.2 The exit of the directional Stinger Trail is to the left. Continue straight.

2.5 The entrance to Stinger is to the left. Continue straight. Stinger is the "narrowest" trail in the system and is

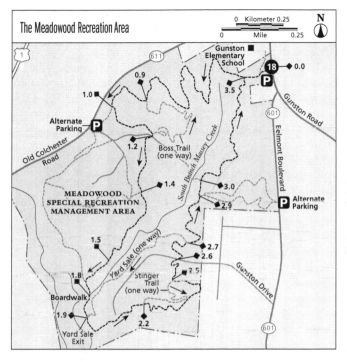

The Meadowood Recreation Area

approximately 0.5 mile long. Turning left here and returning
to this spot will add 0.8 mile to your ride.

2.6 Continue straight through this intersection.

2.7 The entrance to Yard Sale is to the left. Continue straight. Yard
Sale is 0.5 mile long. Turning left here and returning to this
spot will add 1.3 miles to your ride.

2.9 Continue straight through the next two intersections. The trails
to the right will take you to Belmont Boulevard, an alternate
starting point.

3.0 Continue straight through this intersection. The doubletrack to
the left will take you back to the entrance of the Boss Trail.

3.5 Arrive back at the starting point.

Ride Information

BIKE SHOPS
Olde Towne Bicycles Inc., 14477 Potomac Mills Rd.,
Woodbridge, VA 22192; (703) 491-5700; www.oldetowne
bicycles.com

RESTAURANTS
Fair Winds Brewing Company, 7000 Newington Rd.,
Ste. K&L, Lorton, VA 22079; (703) 372-2001; www.fair
windsbrewing.com

Honorable Mentions

There are a few rides that I have not detailed in the book but which I think require at least an honorable mention. In most cases, the rides included in this section are heavily documented and it would be redundant for me to include them in this book. In some cases the rides are also simple out-and-backs or reclaimed rails-to-trails that are easy to follow.

Road and Pathway Honorable Mentions

A. The National Arboretum
The National Arboretum ride is well documented in dozens of publications and websites. You can squeeze out a 9- to 10-mile road loop within the research facilities. The Arboretum is open from 8 a.m. to 5 p.m. daily year-round, except for December 25. Call before you go, (202) 245-2726, because they tend to close the facilities without warning. The roads within the facility are easy to follow and allow you to craft your own loop. For additional information, visit the official National Arboretum website at www.usna.usda.gov.

B. The Anacostia Riverwalk
The Anacostia Riverwalk, also known as the Anacostia River Trail, is a key component of an ongoing effort to revitalize what was once one of our nation's most polluted rivers, the Anacostia. The trail extends from the Tidal Basin in Washington, DC, to just inside the Maryland border to the north. Riders can enjoy up to 20 miles of paved paths along both sides of the Anacostia River and along the way visit some key historic locations, including the Navy Yard, Nationals Park, RFK Stadium, Anacostia Park, and

Diamond Teague Park. For additional information, visit the Capitol Riverfront website at www.capitolriverfront.org/go/anacostia-riverwalk-trail.

C. The Chesapeake and Ohio Canal (C&O Canal)

The C&O Canal is another heavily documented route that runs from Georgetown in DC to Cumberland, Maryland. Feasibly you could ride this path all the way to Pittsburgh, Pennsylvania. You can access the C&O from the same starting point as the Capital Crescent Trail ride along the Georgetown waterfront. If you are interested, the National Park Service website (www.nps.gov) offers comprehensive information on the canal.

D. The N.W. Branch Trail

The N.W. Branch is actually two trails. The first is a hard-surface trail that extends from the Capital Beltway in the southeastern portion of Montgomery County to Prince George's County and connects with the Anacostia Tributary Trail System. The natural-surface portion of the trail north of the Beltway has been recently opened to bikes, and several new trails have been built along the banks of the creek and the adjacent hillsides. The trails are not easy, but if you are up to the challenge, and are ready to test your climbing legs and experience some modern flow trails, I highly suggest you take a look. The unpaved trails continue north beyond Colesville Road and parallel the creek. If paved rolling paths are more your speed, then I suggest you try the clearly marked and easy-to-follow out-and-back trail. You can combine it with the Sligo Creek Trail to create a longer ride. For additional information, visit the Montgomery Parks website at www.montgomeryparks

.org/parks-and-trails/northwest-branch-stream-valley-park/
rachel-carson-greenway-northwest-branch-stream-valley-
park-trails.

E. The Indian Head Rail Trail

Located in southern Maryland is the 13-mile Indian Head
Rail Trail (IHRT). The trail connects the town of Indian
Head with US 301 in White Plains in Charles County. For
more information on this trail, visit the Charles County,
Maryland, website at www.charlescountymd.gov/Home/
Components/FacilityDirectory/FacilityDirectory/76/.

F. Sligo Creek Trail

The Sligo Creek Trail is another regional bike trail that follows Sligo Creek from central Montgomery County to the
border of Prince George's County. The trail is simply an
out-and-back from Wheaton Regional Park in Montgomery
County to New Hampshire Avenue along the Prince George's
County border. It is approximately 8.5 miles in length, well-
marked, and easy to follow. For additional information
and maps of the trail, visit the Montgomery Parks website
at www.montgomeryparks.org/parks-and-trails/sligo-creek
-stream-valley-park/sligo-creek-stream-valley-trail.

G. The Washington and Old Dominion Trail, the
Custis Trail, and Four Mile Run

In my description of the Mount Vernon Trail (MVT), I
refer to it as one of several backbone trails in the region.
The Washington and Old Dominion Trail (W&OD), or
"the WOD," is one of these. The WOD can be ridden in
its entirety from Shirlington in Arlington to Purcellville in
Loudoun County. The paved trail extends for nearly 45 miles

through Virginia's countryside and offers a great challenge to any rider. For more information, visit the Northern Virginia Regional Park Authority website at www.nvrpa.org/park/w_od_railroad and the Friends of the W&OD Trail website at www.wodfriends.org.

The WOD is a great recreational trail but also serves as an important regional commuter corridor; sadly, its terminus in Shirlington falls short of Washington, DC. However, most commuters have the option of connecting the WOD with another popular regional trail, the Martha Custis Trail. Unlike the WOD, which is a reclaimed rail bed and relatively flat, the Custis Trail parallels I-66 and has several moderate climbs. The trail is also considerably shorter, at just 4 miles, but despite that is one of the most popular and used trails in the region. Its connectivity to both the WOD and the MVT have made it a critical link for cyclists looking to extend their rides, and for commuters who need to access the District.

Like the Custis Trail, Four Mile Run is another critical link in the region's trail network. For many, this trail is simply an extension of the WOD. The paved trail parallels the WOD from just north of US 50 in Arlington until the WOD ends in Shirlington. From there, Four Mile Run continues along the watershed until it intersects with the Mount Vernon Trail. Like the Custis Trail, it provides a critical link for commuters making their way into the District and for recreational riders wishing to extend their rides. For more information on Four Mile Run, visit the Arlington County Parks website at https://parks.arlingtonva.us/locations/four-mile-run-park/.

Mountain Bike Honorable Mentions

H. Black Hill Regional Park

Black Hill Regional Park is situated in the northern part of Montgomery County. Black Hill is home to mountain biking, hiking, horseback riding, boating, fishing, and more.

Upon entering the park, visitors are treated to an outstanding view of Little Seneca Lake. The lake was built through the partnership of the Maryland-National Capital Park and Planning Commission and the Washington Suburban Sanitary Commission. Its design marked it as a dual-purpose lake, providing both recreation and an emergency water supply for the Washington metropolitan area. In addition to nearly 8 miles of singletrack mountain bike trails, the park also has a 4.3-mile paved cycling path. Access to other natural-surface trails, including Ten Mile Creek and the Hoyles Mill Connector, provides a multitude of opportunities to extend your rides. Black Hill Regional Park, along with many other mountain bike trails in the Montgomery County region, is detailed in my other guide, *Mountain Biking the Washington D.C./Baltimore Area*. For additional information visit the the Montgomery Parks website at www.montgomeryparks.org/parks-and-trails/black-hill-regional-park.

I. Lake Fairfax Park

Located in the growing business and population center of Reston, Virginia, is Lake Fairfax Park, a 476-acre park that serves thousands of people per day, including a growing number of cyclists along its 10-plus miles of trails. In addition to a diverse network of trails that cater to cyclists of all abilities, the park is home to northern Virginia's first pump track. The park boasts multiple athletic fields, campgrounds, picnic shelters, a carousel, and a skate park surrounding a gorgeous 20-acre lake. Visit the official Lake Fairfax Park website at www.fairfaxcounty.gov/parks/lake-fairfax.

J. Cedarville State Forest

Cedarville State Forest includes a wonderful network of wooded trails and dirt roads that guides visitors beneath tall stands of loblolly and white pine, around groves of holly and magnolia trees, past a 4-acre lake, through the headwaters of Maryland's largest freshwater swamp, and across abandoned farmland with streams and springs once used for making moonshine. This is a wonderful ride for novices and experts alike who have a passion for the great outdoors. Cedarville's terrain is mostly flat, as is most of southern Maryland, but the beauty of its wooded forest roadways rises high above most everything else in the area.

Area Clubs and Advocacy Groups

Here is a short list of the many organizations that make the Washington, DC, region a great place to ride a bike.

Bike Arlington
www.bikearlington.com
Bike Arlington offers bike education and encouragement. Its mission is to make it easy to get around Arlington by bike.

Bike Maryland
www.bikemaryland.org
Bike Maryland represents all bicyclists in its efforts to create a state that's fun and safe to ride in.

Capital Bikeshare
www.capitalbikeshare.com
Pick up a bike at one of hundreds of stations around the metro DC area.

Fairfax Alliance for Better Bicycling
https://fabb-bikes.org
A volunteer organization that works to make bicycling fun, safe, and accessible for people of all ages in Fairfax County, Virginia.

League of American Bicyclists
www.bikeleague.org
The League of American Bicyclists represents bicyclists in the movement to create safer roads, stronger communities, and a bicycle-friendly America.

Maryland Interscholastic Cycling League
https://marylandmtb.org
The Maryland Interscholastic Cycling League was organized in 2017 to provide a fun, safe, and high-quality mountain biking program for students in grades 6 to 12.

Mid-Atlantic Off-Road Enthusiasts (MORE)
https://more-mtb.org
MORE is a nonprofit organization representing thousands of Washington, DC, Maryland, and northern Virginia mountain bikers.

Washington Area Bicycle Association (WABA)
https://waba.org
WABA envisions a region in which biking is joyful, safe, popular, and liberating; supported by the necessary infrastructure, laws, activities, and investments; and where bicycle ridership mirrors the incredible diversity of our communities.

Ride Index

About the Author

Martín Fernández's love for cycling goes way back, but it really flourished when he was in the US Army and stationed at Fort Myer along the perimeter of Arlington National Cemetery. "Those early-morning PT rides through Arlington National Cemetery and over the Memorial Bridge, then onto the National Mall, really cemented my love for the sport. Seeing the mist rise from the Potomac and riding along some of the most iconic monuments and memorials in the nation's capital, with only my breath to keep me company, made me appreciate and love the sites that this city and its surrounding areas have to offer. There is no greater pleasure than exploring your home aboard two wheels." During that time Martín also found the joys of off-road cycling and became heavily involved with the Mid-Atlantic Off-Road Enthusiasts (MORE).

Martín is a Level 1 PMBIA (Professional Mountain Bike Instructors Association) Instructor.

Learn more about Martín, including more of the places he loves to ride, at www.bestridesdc.com.